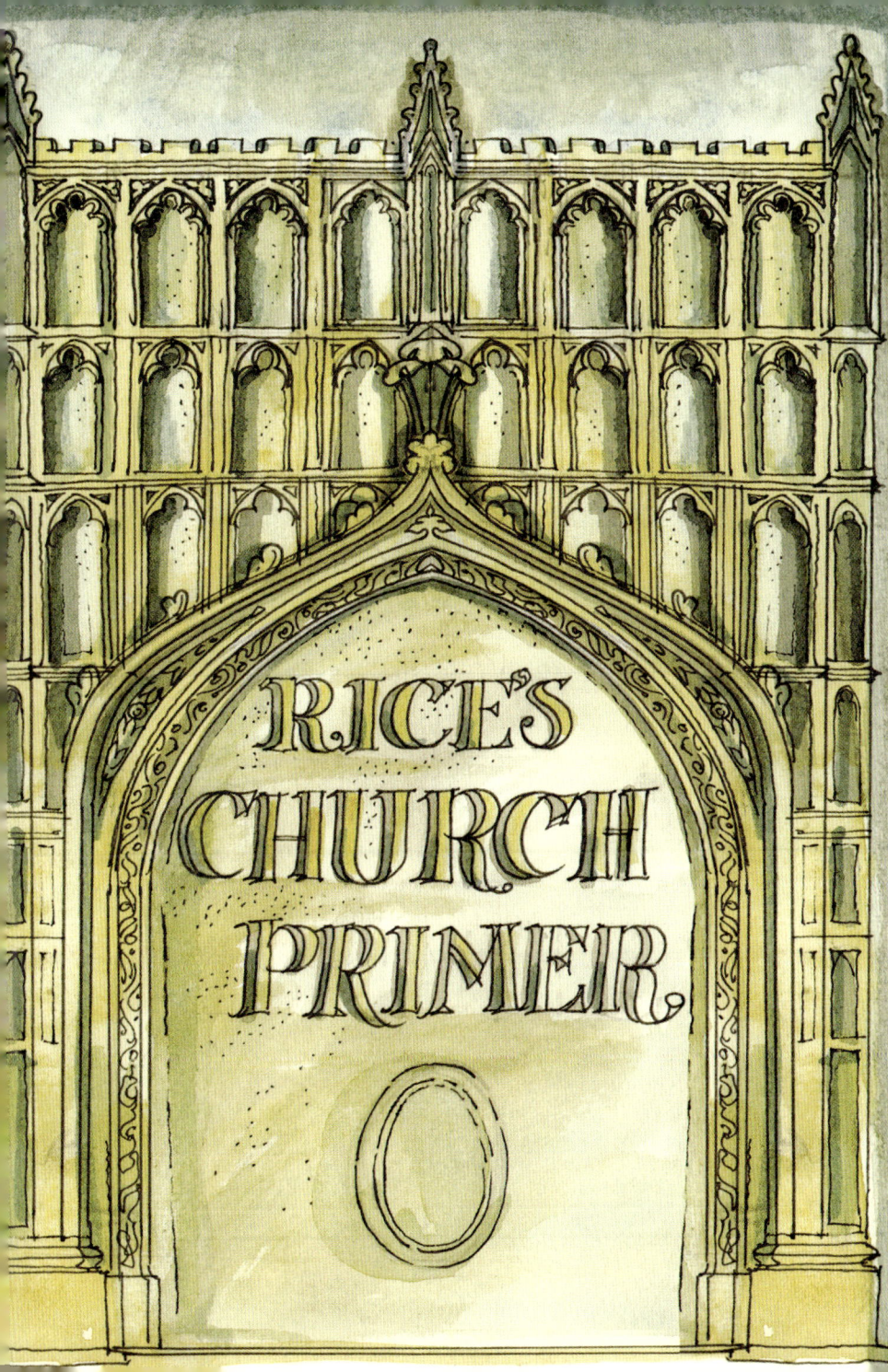

RICE'S
CHURCH
PRIMER

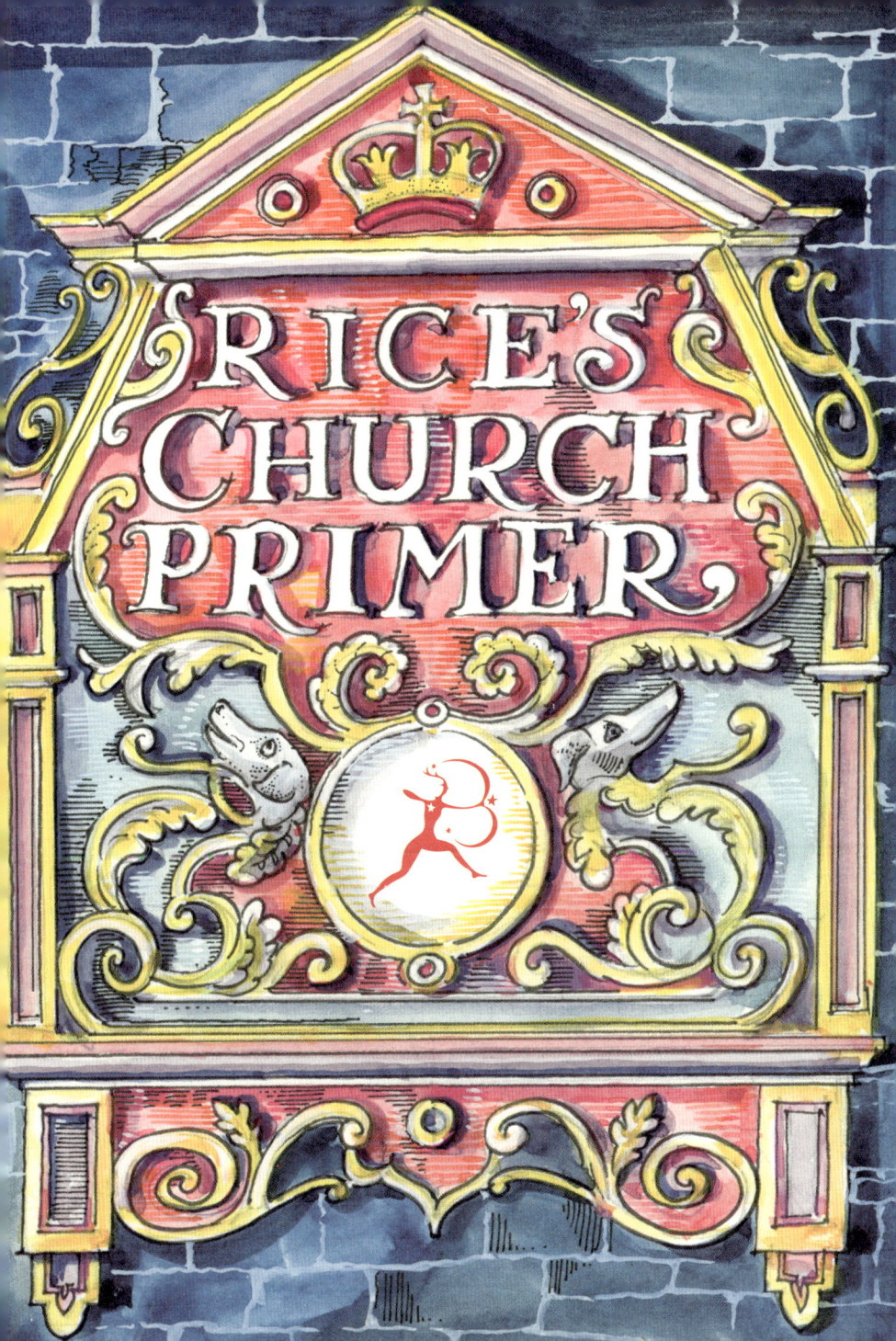

RICE'S CHURCH PRIMER,

For Michael with love

First published in Great Britain 2013

Copyright © 2013 by Matthew Rice

Expanded from a series of architectural cribs commissioned by
and published in *Country Life*.

The moral right of the author has been asserted.

Bloomsbury Publishing Plc
50 Bedford Square
London WC1B 3DP

Bloomsbury Publishing, London, New Delhi, New York and Sydney

A CIP catalogue record for this book is available from the British Library.

ISBN 978 1 4088 0752 1

10 9 8 7 6 5 4 3 2 1

Designer: Peter Dawson, www.gradedesign.com

Printed and bound in China by C&C Offset Printing Co. Ltd.

All papers used by Bloomsbury Publishing are natural, recyclable products
made from wood grown in well-managed forests. The manufacturing
processes conform to the environmental regulations of the country of origin.

www.bloomsbury.com/matthewrice

INTRODUCTION

Churches come in different models, NORMAN ones, GOTHIC ones, CLASSICAL ones, and some in what seems at first like a baffling combination. This Primer is a crib, a shorthand history of church-building, and it is mainly concerned with the naming of parts. It explains the components and features from the major periods of church-building, many of which cross over. These periods are divided into: Saxon and Norman, Early English, Decorated, Perpendicular, Baroque, Georgian, Regency and Early Victorian, High Victorian, and Modern.

Mainly, the Primer is there as an easy reference book which, while editing out a lot of the more esoteric details, is an introduction to the language of church architecture – the GRAMMAR of basic components that reappear again and again, and the VOCABULARY of features from particular periods.

The language of a subject is central to understanding it. Terminology is not a boffinish obsession, but a vital shorthand for describing something, a building in this case, in a way that others can understand. And precision is good. Good because a church is a series of decisions, not of vague ideas. You cannot sketch in limestone or imply in oak. You must consider, weigh up and then take the plunge; a total commitment to that decision is inevitable. The great cathedrals that cost as much as a small war to build are like libraries in terms of the number of decisions they contain. Yet, without the words to describe those decisions, they will remain a closed book. Unlocking that is the purpose of the Primer.

The parish church has an important function, apart from being the focus of religious observance, or a repository of local history (the graves and monuments, the chantry bequests and reserved pews, the register of deaths, baptisms and marriages). It is the best building in the village. Indeed, it is often the only building with a significant listed status in its parish.

The bombing of Britain during the Second World War alerted the nation to the importance of recording and protecting its best buildings. As part of the 1947 Town and Country Planning Act, a series of listing grades were established and allocated to certain buildings: they ranged from I down to II* and then II. Today, there are about ten thousand Grade I buildings and just over twenty thousand that are Grade II*. A great proportion of these are churches; indeed, 45 per cent of Grade I-listed buildings are places of worship. Nikolaus Pevsner's *Buildings of England* (1951–74), the twentieth-century Domesday Book, adds flesh to the bones of that list. It describes, analytically, ALMOST SCIENTIFICALLY, the buildings of architectural significance in every village, the lion's share of each entry being reserved for the parish church.

Listing may be a twentieth-century phenomenon, but the outstanding bestness of a church is not. The cost of construction, the implied hours of human work, the FLIGHTS OF FANCY of its builders and the horizon of their influences make the church and, more still, the abbey, priory or cathedral, the most significant work of art in its surroundings. In fact, it towers over everything. Until the change of focus to secular mansions in the post-Reformation era (from the sixteenth century onwards), the church was the sole canvas for both artists and designers. Even in castles, which competed in terms of expense and social significance, the most intense decoration and creativity was concentrated in the chapel.

The parish church is a dependable reward for visitors today. It is a centuries-old form that has weathered the changes wrought by wealth, empire and industrial revolution. Of course, there are exceptions, mainly the result of INSENSITIVE VICTORIAN RENOVATIONS on pre-existing buildings. And there are instances where the interior of a Modern church is cold and functional, or where the Gothic windows of a medieval building have been replaced, or where tawdry, ill-designed banners and altar cloths from the past fifty years make an ugly smear across older masonry. But, exceptions aside, any church that you visit is likely to be astonishingly beautiful, outshining anything else in the parish.

* * *

'A quiet place' or 'so well loved'. These are the messages written in damp blue biro in the visitors' books of the SIXTEEN THOUSAND PARISH CHURCHES and cathedrals of Britain. Visitors come from the next village, or from London, or perhaps from Auckland or Adelaide, on a pilgrimage to the parish their ancestors left behind in search of something better. But these formulaic comments, although heartfelt and, in some ways, accurate, are only one part of the story. Because churches are also places of violence, discord, despair and grief, discontent and political upheaval, of disrepair and ruin, rebirth and extremist zealotry. For centuries, religion was not only universal and central to our lives, but it was also the focus of the best of British cultural and intellectual expression. Churches represented theatre and cinema, painting and sculpture, literature, illustration, music and philosophy, not to mention education, medicine, travel and politics.

Nowhere is the story of Britain better reflected than in the monuments of an old church. On slabs, biers and plinths, mounted on the wall, or on brasses and graves, the history of this country manifests itself through the story of generations. Nowhere is the progression of architectural history sung more sweetly than in monuments devoted to a single family across the centuries. For example, imagine an amalgam of memorials from churches around the country. Imagine they are devoted to a single family, whom we shall name Harvey:

Sir John Harvey wears helm and broadsword, armour and outlandish spurs, and his feet rest upon a greyhound. He resides in an austere fourteenth-century sarcophagus. Beside him, his wife is hard to read, her face a formulaic mask of inscrutable medieval woman. Perhaps she brought to her marriage a vast income, as well as additions to the much-quartered family shield. Her son, again Sir John, might have directed some of this fortune to weekly masses for her soul, to be said in perpetuity in a custom-built 'chantry' chapel. (In perpetuity until, that is, the REFORMATION swept away the excesses of the Roman Catholic Church in the sixteenth century.)

A modest angel-swoop away from his ancestors, the seventeenth-century Sir John wears a sharp doublet. He has a finely turned calf and a Captain Peacock moustache. His wife lies by his side, as if discussing their many children over a morning cup of tea. Their alabaster sheets, rumpled coldly on the bed, are tucked in with admirable hospital corners. Over them, a sky-diving *putto* with a coronet in his hands is a happy reminder that rank is not forgotten in heaven. Their canopy and bier are swagged and panelled in a romping combination of foreign Classical and native medieval detail. It is like a stone copybook of architectural ornament, summing up the flux and inconsistencies of the era.

On the walls (whitewashed since the Reformation) is the joyless white Carrara-marble record of a later Sir John Harvey's life. It shows that his death in Calcutta in the mid-nineteenth century was mourned by a mother and sister back at home. But perhaps other, unrecorded, tears were shed for him by a MUGHAL BEAUTY in foreign lands. Who knows?

They lie together, the Harveys. And with them lie rectors and their wives, decent farmers who funded loaves for the poor, church wardens and the less-forgotten sons of two World Wars. In this way – through the monuments, tablets and brasses of any church – the continuity as well as the vicissitudes of British history are recorded. A visit to a church is, of course, a visit to a holy place, but because of those Harveys, it is also a way of keying in to local, national and even global history. Their equivalents are there to see across the world; on the walls of Christ Church in Shimla, India (1857), or of the Caribbean St Paul's Church in Charlestown, Nevis (1651).

And the ELEPHANT IN THE ROOM? God. Churches are not village halls, market places or concert halls. Although this is a book about ecclesiastical architecture, the Church is, in truth, devoted to worship, to community and to the marking of local and personal rites of passage. These represent the central theme of every architectural feature and, without them, the Church is dead.

GRAMMAR

The parts shop, or grammar, of church architecture has a BAFFLING NUMBER of components. Some are used, on and off, throughout the ages. Others appear then disappear during the periods in which Classicism rules, or tries to rule, the roost; and still more are introduced then superseded as one Gothic style follows another over the centuries.

The grammar section is the place where ILLUSTRATIONS BEAT DESCRIPTIONS, so the next few pages may be the most important in this book. Everything has a name – every bulge, bump or curve, each decorative device of structural solution can be described. As this is not an academic book, there will still be plenty of terms left on the shelf; divisions of tracery component or other bits of architecture, but only because they cause confusion; wood occluding trees. However, knowing the terms frees one from MUZZY DESCRIPTIONS and lack of clarity, and allows for discussion, so it's worth learning all the basics. Although many of these terms are covered again in following chapters, they are set out here for ready reference.

The inital illustrations concern the plan of churches and are applicable to nearly every era. The nave, chancel with choir, aisles, tower and porch; these are the divisions in ground plan that define the basic parts inside a church, just as the STOREYS and BAYS (subdivisions horizontal and vertical) do externally. Then there are period-led variations – arch shape, windows and their tracery styles, vaulting, timber roofing and buttresses.

Beyond this, there are the details, the vocabulary of an architectural style. Beak-head and chevron are Norman arch decorations; for the three major Gothic periods of architectural style, nail-head and ball-flower define Early English; mouchettes and daggers are subdivisions of Decorated tracery; and depressed arches, shallow cusped trefoils and repeated panelling are the terms in which the Perpendicular style is set.

Under the influence of Inigo Jones in the seventeenth century, the Classical LANGUAGE OF THE ANCIENTS replaces the native

Gothic. Capitals whose garbled Classical references had become overgrown with Celtic foliage and Dark Age bestiaries are again made pure and bright.

The Classical language of orders – Doric, Ionic, Corinthian and Composite – is divided into plinth, foot, shaft, collar and capital on columns; and architrave, frieze and cornice on entabulature. The entabulature is the part of a building that a column supports. These, and the round-topped arch, the pediment, and treatments such as rustication or vermiculation, are the look of the seventeenth and eighteenth centuries. They are, of course, the same elements of which secular buildings are comprised.

Indeed, it was the similarity between church and secular buildings that was perceived by reformers in the nineteenth century as irreligious, ALMOST PROFANE. The language of Julius Caesar, of Zeus and Hera, of Medusa and the sirens was seen as anathema to these pro-Gothic-style reformers of Victorian Oxford and Cambridge. And so the innocuous pediment, the volute and the Vitruvian scroll became symbols of polytheistic and morally corrupt codes and beliefs.

As the nineteenth century's love affair with the Gothic developed a love-blind disregard for history, the mixing-up of traditional architectural elements became desirable. A Venetian Gothic stilted arch with a broken pediment and a terracotta sunflower crammed together would be read as commendable eclecticism. This, together with structural polychromy, which is the use of distinct colour and material variation in a building, was later to attract opprobrium from Classically sympathising Modernists. It was under their influence that so much of Victorian church building was demolished in the middle of the twentieth century.

Really, the next twelve pages of this book are the only bit that is worth learning off by heart to carry you through your church visiting. None of the details are attributed to particular examples; shown in this chapter are the basics only.

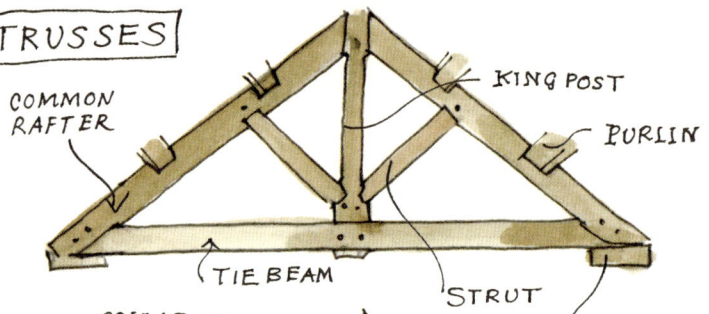

COMMON RAFTER

KING POST

PURLIN

TIE BEAM

STRUT

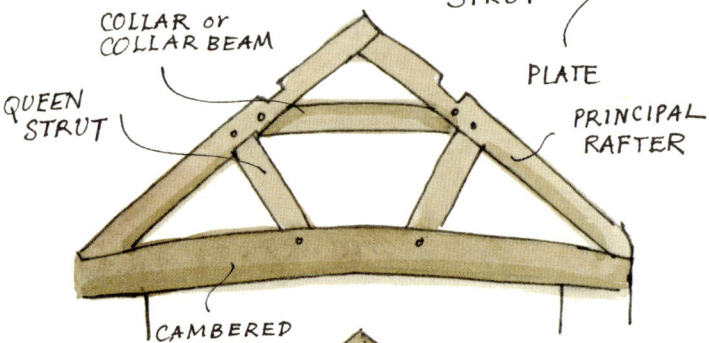

COLLAR or COLLAR BEAM

QUEEN STRUT

PLATE

PRINCIPAL RAFTER

CAMBERED TIE BEAM

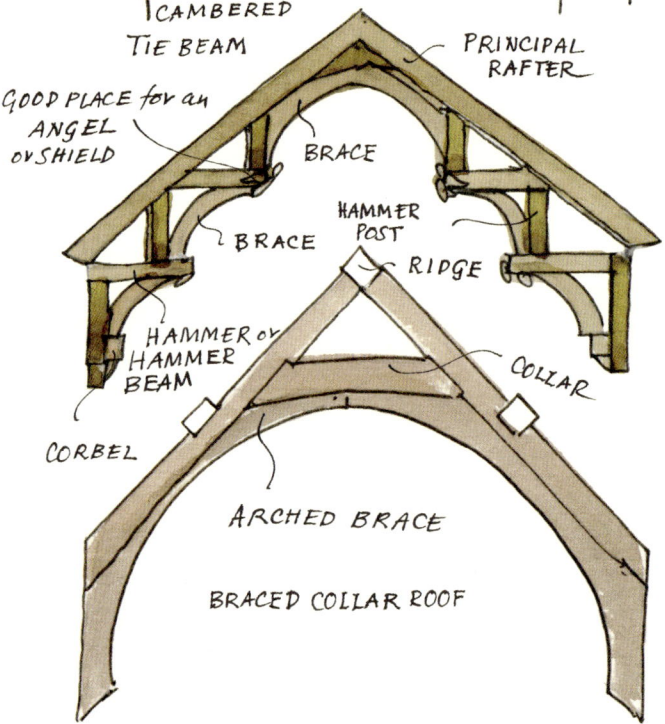

PRINCIPAL RAFTER

GOOD PLACE for an ANGEL or SHIELD

BRACE

BRACE

HAMMER POST

RIDGE

HAMMER or HAMMER BEAM

COLLAR

CORBEL

ARCHED BRACE

BRACED COLLAR ROOF

ARCHES

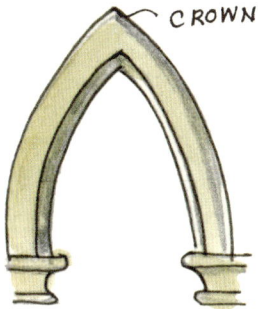

CROWN

LANCET or
POINTED ARCH

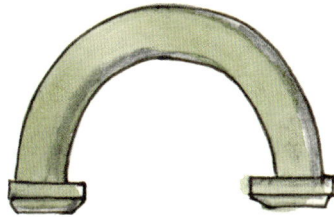

SPRING

SEMI-CIRCULAR, NORMAN
or ROMANESQUE ARCH

FOUR-CENTRED ARCH

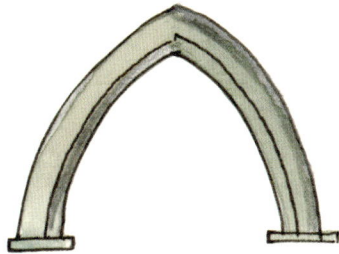

EQUILATERAL ARCH

✳ THESE ARE THE KEY TO THE WHOLE BUSINESS...

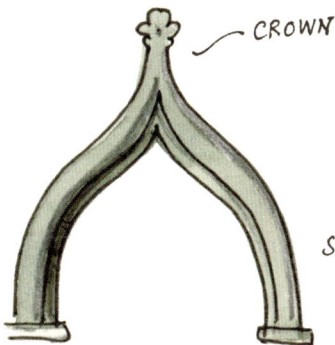

CROWN

OGEE, or OGIVAL
ARCH

STILT...

STILTED ARCH

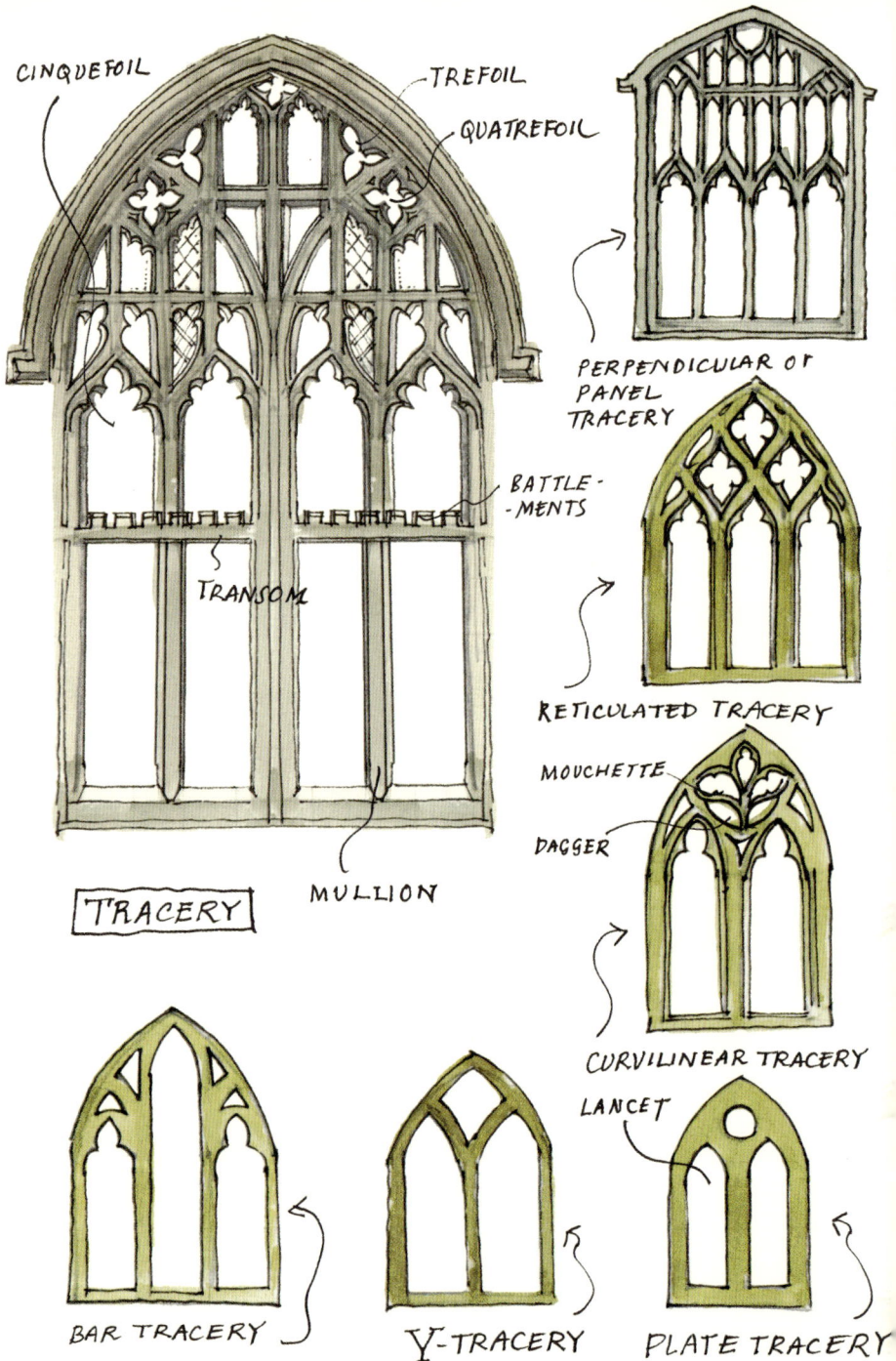

CINQUEFOIL

TREFOIL

QUATREFOIL

BATTLE- -MENTS

TRANSOM

MULLION

TRACERY

PERPENDICULAR or PANEL TRACERY

RETICULATED TRACERY

MOUCHETTE

DAGGER

CURVILINEAR TRACERY

LANCET

BAR TRACERY

Y-TRACERY

PLATE TRACERY

DIAPERING

BATTLEMENT

WEATHER VANE

CROCKETTED FINIAL

CROCKETTED SPIRE

SAXON WINDOW

OCTAGONAL LANTERN

GABLET

LUCARNE

ROUND TOWER

FLYING BUTTRESS

SET-OFF or WEATHER TABLE

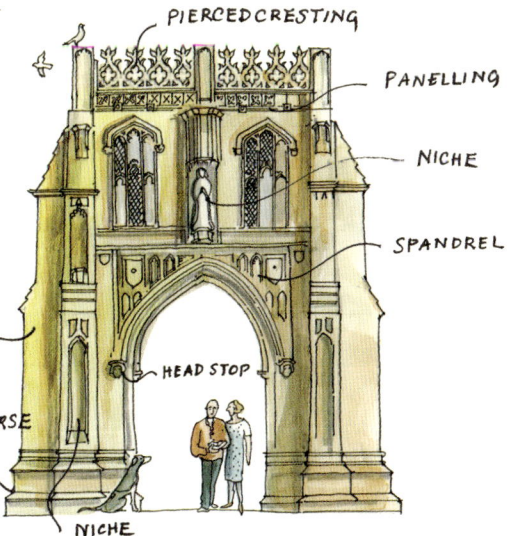

PIERCED CRESTING

PANELLING

NICHE

SPANDREL

BUTTRESS

HEAD STOP

BASE-COURSE

PLINTH

NICHE

NAVE · SANCTUARY

1100

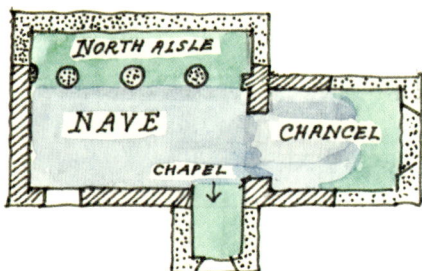

NORTH AISLE · NAVE · CHANCEL · CHAPEL

1250

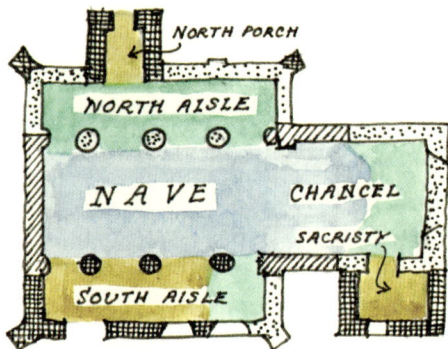

NORTH PORCH · NORTH AISLE · NAVE · CHANCEL · SACRISTY · SOUTH AISLE

1350

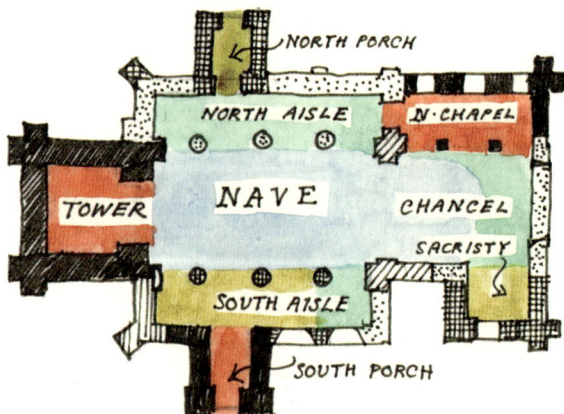

NORTH PORCH · NORTH AISLE · N·CHAPEL · TOWER · NAVE · CHANCEL · SACRISTY · SOUTH AISLE · SOUTH PORCH

1500

CLERESTORY

BALDACCHINO

APSE

ORGAN PIPES

TESTER

PRIEST

ARCADE

LOWSCREEN

LECTERN

ALTAR

PULPIT

ORGAN CONSOLE

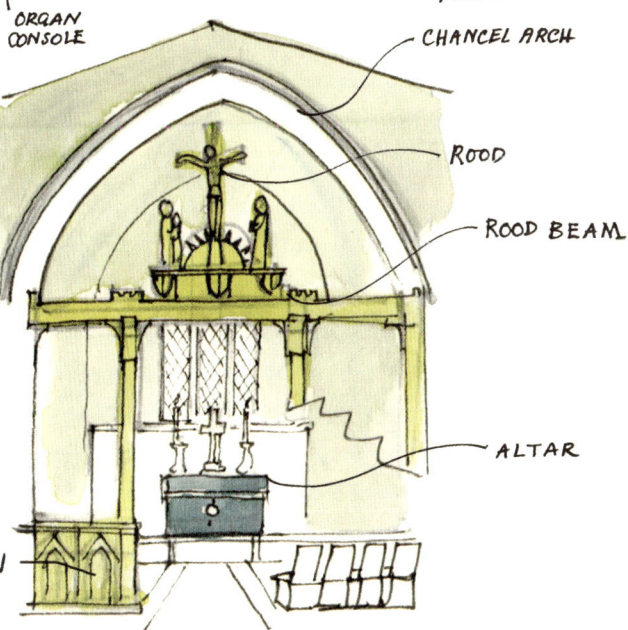

CHANCEL ARCH

ROOD

ROOD BEAM

ALTAR

ROOD SCREEN

BARREL VAULT

GROIN VAULT

ABACUS

GROIN

SPRINGING
(ie from where the
Arch springs)

RIB

CUSHION CAPITAL

QUADRIPARTITE VAULT
(intersecting diagonal
ribs)

VAULT SHAFT

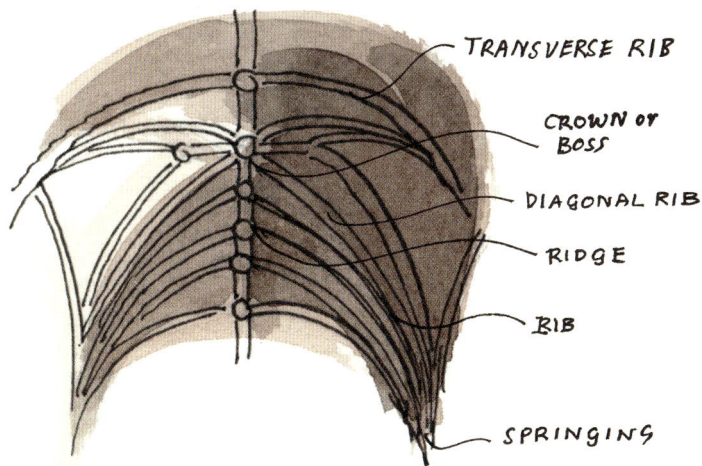

TRANSVERSE RIB

CROWN or BOSS

DIAGONAL RIB

RIDGE

RIB

SPRINGING

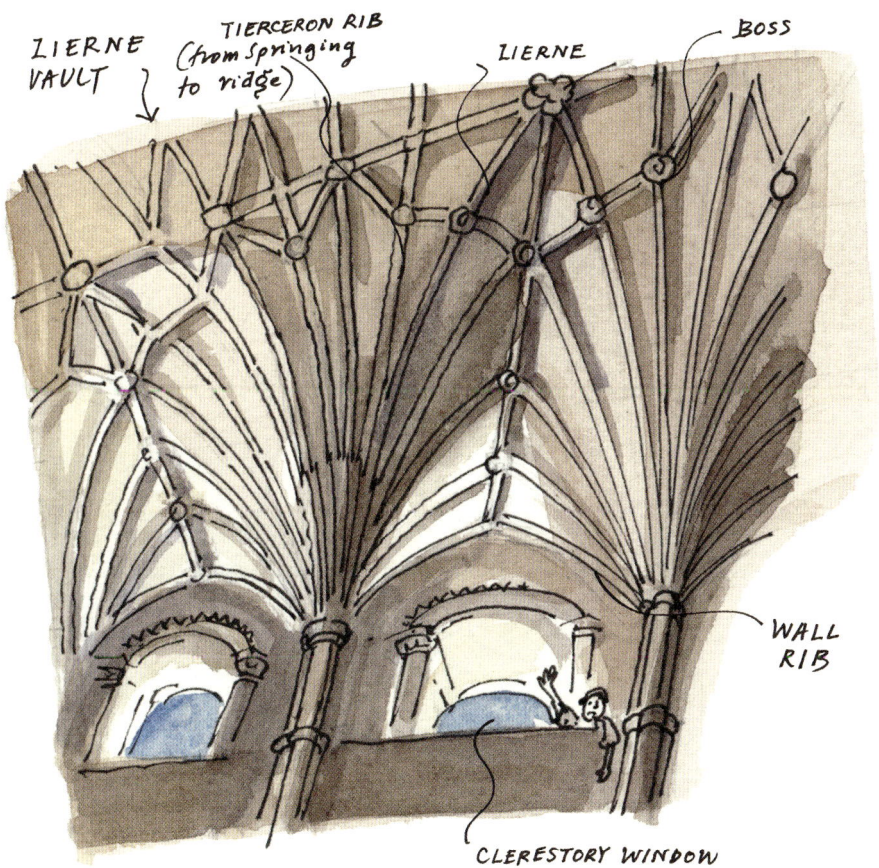

LIERNE VAULT

TIERCERON RIB (from springing to ridge)

LIERNE

BOSS

WALL RIB

CLERESTORY WINDOW

FRIEZE

COLONNADE

COFFER (if in ceiling)

IN PLAN

IN PLAN

IN PLAN

PANEL (if in wall)

PILASTER
(ie less than
50% projecting)

ENGAGED COLU
(self-explanat

COLUMN

RENAISSANCE
BALUSTER

RA

BALUST

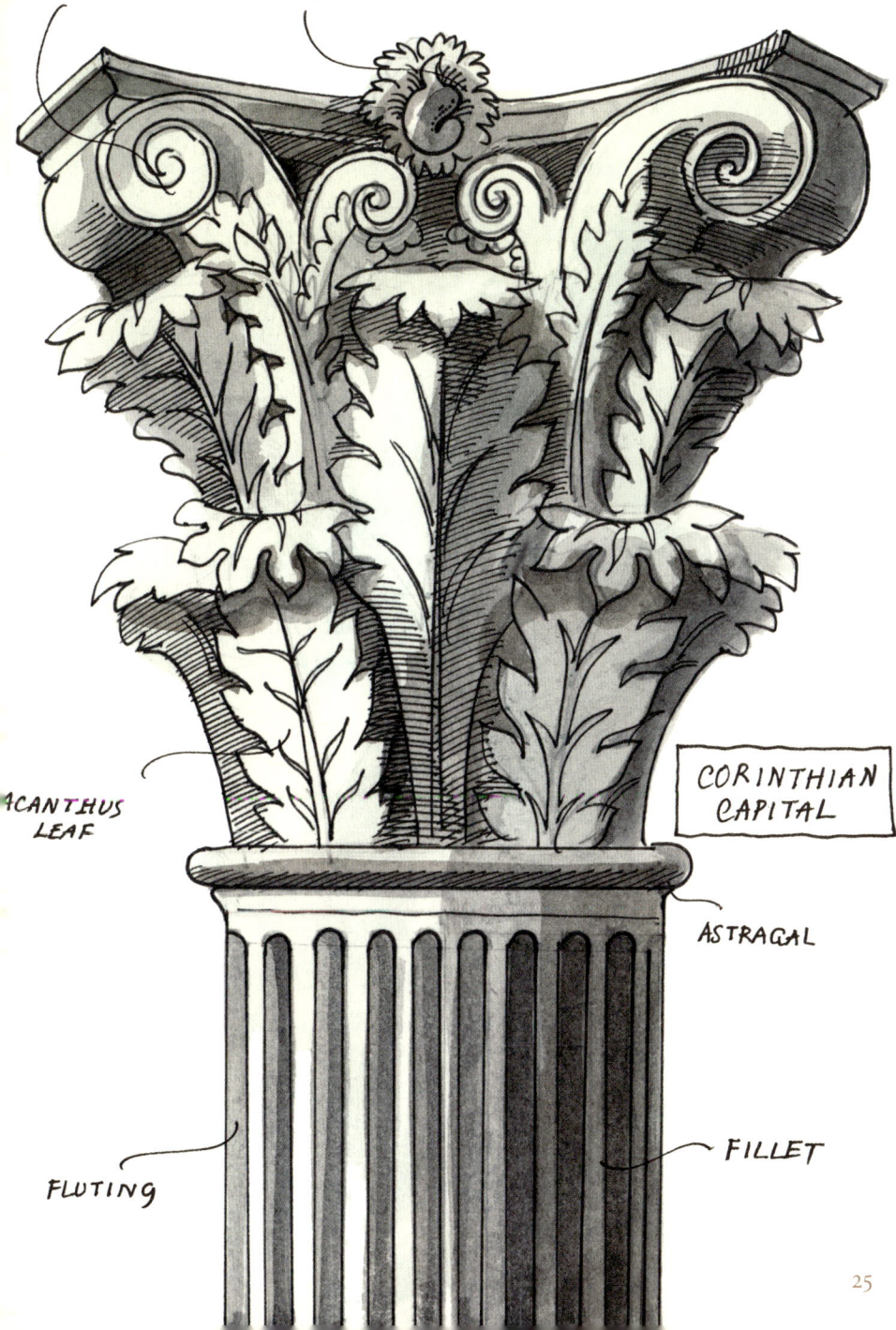

HELIX ᴏʀ VOLUTE   FLEURON

CORINTHIAN
CAPITAL

ACANTHUS
LEAF

ASTRAGAL

FILLET

FLUTING

25

ABACUS

IONIC

EGG & DART

VOLUTE

FLUTE
FILLET

TUSCAN/DORIC

ABACUS

ECHINUS

FILLET

NECK

ASTRAGAL

FILLET

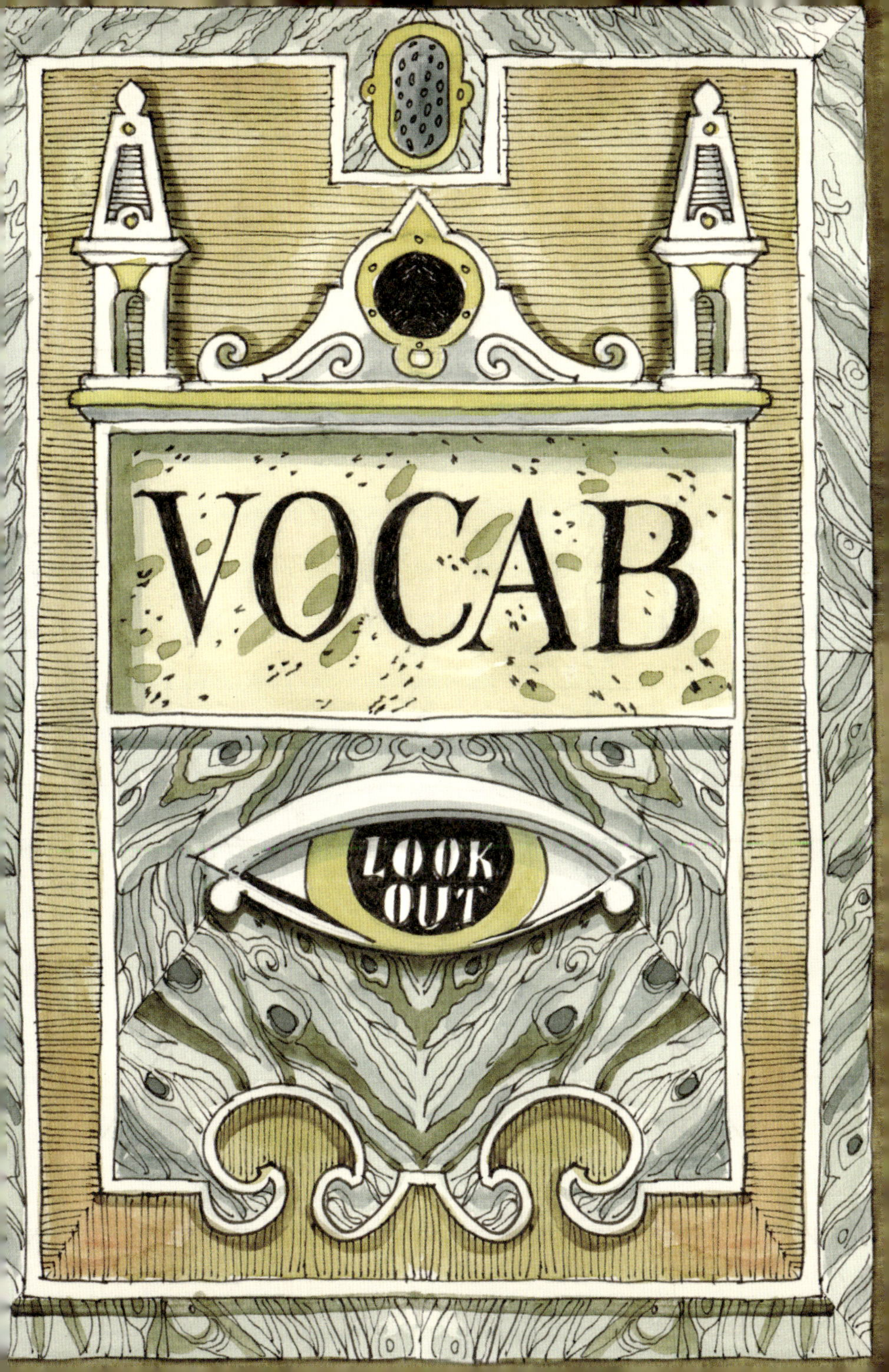
VOCAB
LOOK OUT

SAXON & NORMAN

There is a ROMAN CHURCH in Britain. It is only a few foundations and a fragment of mosaic floor in Silchester in Berkshire (if it really is a church; there is some suggestion that it might be a synagogue, as Christianity was not adopted as the IMPERIAL RELIGION until Emperor Constantine saw the light in 312, yes, AD, as we are talking churches here...). It is our first, and its rather distressed condition is characteristic of almost all pre-Conquest churches, most of which only survive as bits in later buildings.

In 410 the Roman Empire of the West was stabbed fatally. This, our island, was then open to all comers and it was repeatedly invaded by ANGLES, SAXONS and JUTES from Scandinavia and Northern Germany. For the next five hundred years, periods of comparative peaceful settlement were interrupted by violent invasion ('*et eo in tempore nunc cives nunc hostes vincebant*', according to Gildas the monk in his sixth-century work *On The Ruin of Britain*. Loosely translated, it means 'first we were on top and then they were').

The inhabitants spoke – and, in part, still speak – the language that they knew before the Roman centuries. The Jutes formed the kingdom of Kent, the Angles became the North-folk and the South-folk, and the Saxons dwelt in Essex, Sussex and Wessex. A new

Christianity, meanwhile, was entering from the Continent: revitalising monks spread into South Wales and Ireland. These early Christians built little monasteries and erected high crosses. Their lasting architectural achievements date from Ninian's Celtic mission (400) in Galloway and Columba's in Iona (563).

In 597, Pope Gregory the Great sent Augustine from Rome to 'destroy the idols, purify the temples with holy water; set relics there; and let them become temples of the true God, so the people will have no need to change their places of concourse. And where, of old, they were WONT TO SACRIFICE OXEN TO DEMONS, in this matter, also, there should be some substitution of solemnity.'

What a *tour de force* of pragmatism, every aspect covered and turned to the service of the advancing new faith! AUGUSTINE had been prior of a Benedictine monastery where vows of poverty, chastity and obedience were the rule, civilised arts were taught and manual labour required. Accompanied by monks and masons, Augustine must have arrived at Canterbury in full regalia. Wearing the armour of Christ, he converted the king and built his first church out of stone, securing the maintenance of ecclesiastical interests in the Anglo-Saxon state. In the centuries that followed, churches became the centre of what had been pagan Saxon settlements. They had the patronage of the ruling caste; even at parish-church level, they were the highest-status buildings in the village.

The VENERABLE BEDE OF JARROW, an eighth-century monk and chronicler, and once a staple of school history books, wrote that a bishop's chief work was to preach. He referred to the life of the archbishop Theodore, who had ordained priests, and instituted teachers to devote themselves to preaching, baptising and celebrating the Sacred Mysteries in places too far away for a bishop to reach. As little distinction was made between secular and sacred, between Church and State, local priests came to represent the governmental agent on the spot. They were the civilising authority.

The church buildings from which they operated, however, remained unregimented. Typically, no Saxon corner is really a right angle, and walls are neither parallel nor of equal length. There were variations from north to south in Anglo-Saxon churches. In the eighth century, the prosperous and accomplished Celtic North produced the crosses of Bewcastle and Ruthwell, and the Lindisfarne Gospels. These use cursive and often SINISTER CELTIC MOTIFS that draw on the Norse antecedents of their builders. The South showed closer links to Rome. The tenth-century internal window at Deerhurst, Gloucestershire, has fluted, even reeded pilasters that make a backwards reference to the culture of our old imperial masters – a feature that would not appear again for five hundred years.

The connection to Rome survived in a more general way in the basilica ground plan. This plan, used in churches in early Christian Rome, for example Santa Maria in Trastevere (1143), derives from the Roman law-court formula of a large simple hall, later known as the NAVE, with aisles on either side. At one end there was an APSE in which a judge or magistrates might sit. In many ancient sites, those of the Byzantine Empire in the East in particular, the building was entered through a full-width anteroom, or NARTHEX. In churches, this area would develop into the porch, which played a significant religious role in later centuries.

Churches in the South of Britain often had a CHANCEL leading out of a nave which gave onto north and south porticos. At Bradford-upon-Avon, there is a Saxon church with a charming nave and tiny chancel so self-effacing as to be lost for centuries inside a house.

If not of timber, church buildings were made of rag or rubble and, sometimes, reused Roman bricks (brick-making was a lost skill in the eighth century). Windows and doors had triangular tops, with roughly carved outsize elements framing doorways; thirteenth-century St Peter's in Britford, Wiltshire, boasts a fragment of Classically inspired vine decoration, showing that the ECHOES OF ROMAN EUROPE still whispered on.

Most of the achievement so far mentioned was once again demolished in the Viking raids of the ninth century. The Dark Ages on our island were VERY DARK. Pagan attacks, rape, slaughter and general mayhem overtook the Saxon kingdom. During King Alfred the Great's reign from 871, however, social order was restored.

NORMAN architecture is a branch of the Western style called ROMANESQUE, one of the great phases of the world's architecture. When Edward the Confessor, THE LAST SAXON KING, returned from a long exile in France in the first quarter of the eleventh century, he brought with him both craftsmen and ecclesiastics from Normandy, and a vision of Romanesque architecture. When he founded Westminster Abbey in 1065, it was longer, with its twelve bays, than his French models and it marked the beginning of something much bigger to come.

The Norman invader William the Conqueror's triumph in 1066 marked the beginning of five hundred years of continuous progress. The massive muscularity of Norman building was not only a stylistic change of tone, but a physical manifestation of the Normans' heavy-handed MARTIAL RULE. The almost frightening force of Peterborough Cathedral is, like the castles built around the country, an expression of power. The knights who charged and thundered to victory at Hastings were bishops as well as barons. The conquered Saxons must have looked on, astonished, as tremendous stones were cut, carved and hoisted aloft. It was not monastic contemplation and meditation that characterised and brought about the vast building programme in England; churches were a weapon of occupation.

The new cathedrals were spaces of colour and light. Our impression of Norman church and cathedral interiors as places of grey austerity was unknown then. Ely Cathedral, now empty of chairs and lacking paint, manifests for us a satisfying form of monochrome beauty and noble lines of architecture, but originally these would have been broken by bands of bright paint and the glint of metal, peopled by priests wearing elaborate Byzantine-style vestments and jewels.

The Normans built thick walls that were unlike the thin and well-mortared walls of Saxon churches. This search for stability and support brought with it features such as nave arcades, buttresses and hollow walls. The development of building techniques was a pattern of trial and error, experiment and sometimes collapse. The massive crossing tower is a recurrent feature and there are not-always-achieved plans for two west towers on either side of a great façade; this format, much used in Europe since Charlemagne's imperial chapels, is known as a westworks.

The dictionary of Romanesque decoration is lavish: zigzag, billet reel, pellet, cable, lozenge, interlacing ornament and knotwork. And sometimes there is a flashback, a revisiting of wild-eyed creatures and the threatening repeated beak-head motifs, symbols not of the wrath of God, but of the axe-wielding fury of the Vikings who had once conquered not only England but, only two hundred years previously, both Normandy and Sicily too.

Biblical scenes are displayed on capitals, and a series of formalised repeated borders are added, some geometric, some (such as the waterleaf motif) more natural; all deeply cut. Shafts rise up walls to spring arches, barrel vaults and groin vaults. Meanwhile, FONTS replace baptisteries: these are initially in the form of a wooden tub, which later develops into a stone bowl, then into a bowl on four columns cylindrical, hexagonal or octagonal, and then, finally, into the rare, square, master craftsman's Tournai marble (1150) featuring animals and St Nicholas, the kindly children's saint, at Winchester Cathedral.

Durham Cathedral (begun 1093) lowers over the River Wear. It is massive and powerful. Inventive and highly accomplished, Christian Northumberland was for a time a centre of the Arts. The accurate cutting of building-stone, the improvement of mortar, the vast cylindrical columns, their deeply incised decoration, the advance from axe to hammer-and-chisel for sculpting – all this was progress. Most significantly, the bold decision to vault the nave in stone rather than build a wooden roof was to become a template for the next great phase of building, Early English.

ST MATTHEW'S · LANGFORD
OXFORDSHIRE · C. 1080
(PARAPET & CORBEL TABLE 1200)

ST BARTHOLOMEW'S
FINGEST · BUCKS

ROUND~TOPPED
WINDOWS/ BELL
OPENING

LESENE

BELFRY

LOUVRE

STRING
COURSE

ROMANESQUE
RELIEF

QUOINS/
LONG & SHORT
WORK

LATER GOTHIC
WINDOW

T ANDREW'S. SOUTH LOPHAM
ORFOLK · C.1100 · PEVSNER SAYS
MOST POWERFUL NORMAN TOWER
SIBLE from AFAR "

VE-STOREY TOWER ⟶

BATTLEMENTS are LATER

BIRKIN · YORKSHIRE

CORBEL TABLE

BLIND ARCADING

CLASPING
BUTTRESS

TOURNAI MARBLE FONT

NARROW CHANCEL

NORMAN CHALICE

CLOISONNÉ RELIQUARY
MADE IN LIMOGES

CABOCHON

LION'S-HEAD BRASS
KNOCKER

ST
THOMAS OF CANTERBURY'S MARTYRDOM

PAINTED ARCH · ALL·SAINTS
DOWN AMPNEY ·GLOUCESTERSHIRE

ST MICHAEL WEIGHING SOULS...

HORSE-
-SHOE
CAPITAL

MOULDINGS

BILLET (ROUND) BILLET (SQUARE) CHEVRON CABLE ou ROPE

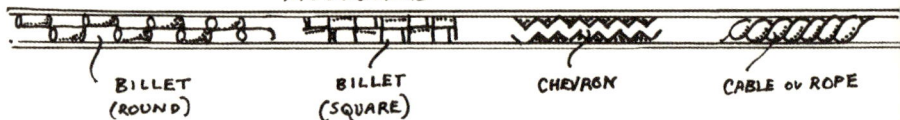

TYMPANUM of MALMESBURY ABBEY · WILTSHIRE 1160

ANGELS SUPPORTING CHRIST

POINTED ARCH

ALL SAINTS
BRIXWORTH
NORTHAMPTONSHIRE
(AN EARLIER BUILDING,
A SAXON MINSTER)

ST MATTHEW'S·LANGFORD
OXFORDSHIRE

(ODDLY RE-SET
COMPONENTS ...)

ST PETER'S
CHARNEY BASSETT
OXFORDSHIRE

KEYSTONE

VOUSSOIRS

ST MARY'S
DEERHURST
GLOUCESTERSHIRE
(10)

POINTED
SAXON ARCH

REEDED
FLUTING

FOUR FINE ROUND-TOPPED WINDOWS

VIKING VIGOUR ⤴ BEASTLY + BEAK-HEAD CARVING

TRUMPETS

VARIOUS ROMANESQUE CAPITALS

AN ACANTHUS
LEAF SURVIVING
IN COLD NORMAN
DAYS

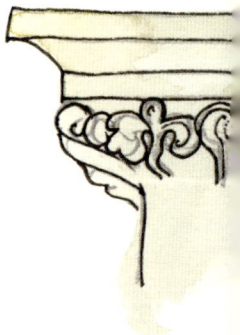

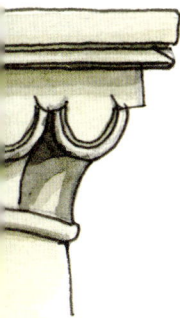

ST LAWRENCE'S
ALTON
HAMPSHIRE

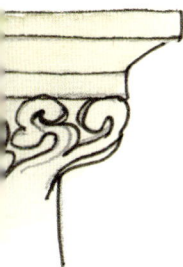

ST ANDREW'S
STOGURSEY
SOMERSET

EARLY ENGLISH

Thomas Rickman, the early-nineteenth-century architectural historian, named three visually defined styles of GOTHIC architecture: Early English, Decorated and Perpendicular. But these terms were not universally adopted – the Victorian Gothicist Augustus Pugin persisted in referring to this first period as the 'pointed' style. His label made clear the defining difference between the round-topped arches of Norman-era Classicism and the pointed arches of the Gothic style which then developed.

Despite its name, the Early English style stems from France. Its roots are to be found in the 1137 rebuilding of St Denis, Paris, by the Abbot Suger (rhymes with Pooh Bear), whose innovations inspired the hilltop cathedral of Laon, Picardy (1160–74). There are significant developments from the Norman cathedrals; here, the walls are no longer massive or thick. Due to superior engineering, they remain structurally sound, despite being sometimes hoisted upon rows of slender columns. The outwards-expanding power of the French kingdom, with Paris at its centre, spread the new lighter style of architecture, with its sophisticated methods of vaulting, arches, stone-cutting and design, throughout the regions of Picardy, Champagne and Normandy.

But why are we discussing France? Because, of course, the many connections between England and its erstwhile invaders, the Norman French, were durable and significant. French was, at the beginning of this period, still spoken at Court and individual craftsmen worked in both places. So the pointed Gothic style crossed the Channel and became Early English. Here, the GUILDS of the medieval towns organised the network of craftsmen and merchants, and regulated the quality of craftsmanship. They maintained excellence through the training of apprentices. Merchants attended markets and fairs, which promoted discussion and cooperation with distant peers. Where the activity of the merchant and the craftsman was held in balance, ideas and competition were spread, stimulating the development of architecture.

Rule from Rome gave the Church a unified structure and a common language in the form of Latin. Feeding into this was the far more exotic influence of the Crusaders, who ventured into the EAST and brought back Oriental notions, ambitions and treasures. In addition, the Code of Chivalry – literary and cultural LINGUA FRANCA of the pan-European nobility who rode across two continents to the Holy Land – introduced elevated ideals of womanhood. This was perhaps implicit in the new cult of the Virgin Mary's worship, which promoted the service of the strong to help the weak and to defend the Church.

The correspondingly far-reaching aspirations of monastery and cathedral builders led to the astonishing and rapid development of the Gothic arch, which enabled them to reach towards the heights with soaring vaulted structures. Whereas the French stressed the vertical, Heaven-reaching visual effect of these newly possible features (in the case of towering cathedrals such as Chartres, rebuilt after a fire in 1194), in England, length and horizontality prevailed. Particularly striking in this respect are the western exterior screens at the cathedrals of Wells (1239) and Lincoln (from 1192), both of which disguise the form of the interior beneath a façade of horizontal decoration peopled with hundreds, even thousands of figures.

Stylistically, the dominant features of Early English are clustered shafts – groupings of thin columns to give an impression of lightness to a fairly massive shaft – and the use of patterns such as nail-head and ball-flower decorating the steeply pointed Gothic arches. Fairly naturalistic, but stylised STIFF-LEAF carving on the capitals (topmost part) of columns was popular. This was to be much emulated in the nineteenth-century Gothic Revival. The pointed lancet is another essential ingredient of the Early English style. It is a tall, narrow, pointed window. How tall and how narrow is dictated by the interests of pattern and of light. The light shining through the window was diffused and coloured by stained or painted glass.

The great intellectual and spiritual development of the twelfth and thirteenth centuries drew on the austerity of St Bernard's Cistercian reforms, the humane charity of St Francis and the philosophy of St Thomas Aquinas. It was the rapid spread of Cistercian monasteries in England that brought to the nation an understanding of the new Early English style, both in spirit and in construction. The solemnity of this strict Benedictine order of monks was reflected in simpler, more severe plans and elevations without INDULGENT DECORATION. Chancels became longer, with straight ends, and the chapels in the transept were squared and screened off.

The first Cistercian House in England had been founded in 1128 at Waverley, Surrey, by the Bishop of Winchester. Yorkshire, still suffering from the devastation caused by William the Conqueror when he put down the revolt of the Northern kingdoms, was ripe for resettlement, and new monasteries thrived in the area's remote spots. Impressive ruins of these large monastic establishments can be found at Byland, Fountains and Rievaulx in Yorkshire.

In autumn 1174, fire broke out in some houses by the gate to the precincts of Canterbury Cathedral. Imagine the horror of the

Benedictine monks as their glorious choir was engulfed. The damage done, the governing Chapter was advised by master-mason William of Sens that the pillars and all they supported had to be removed, but the incumbent monks instructed Sens to rebuild on the original Norman ground plan. Nonetheless, an innovative architectural form was introduced from Laon: a triforium. This was a gallery on the second floor, built into the thickness of the nave wall of the church. The chapel was enlivened by shafts made from Purbeck marble (a shiny dense dark brown limestone from Dorset) set against the lighter Caen stone, whilst the bays were linked in pairs with sexpartite vaults.

Vaulting is complicated and hard to understand, and descriptions of it are, to be honest, a little boring, but it is central to medieval church architecture so you'll just have to get your head round it. Stick with it; it'll be over in ten minutes.

A Norman roof, or BARREL VAULT, is a long half-cylinder of stone that stands on top of the nave walls, leaning heavily on them and exerting outward pressure; the walls need to be massive to withstand the strain. The barrel vault consists of segmental stones spanning the distance between parallel walls, every stone sharing the load.

Where two stone half-cylinders meet one another at right angles, for example where a nave meets with a transept, the result is a GROIN VAULT. Like the ancient Romans, the Normans used semi-circular arches, each arch's height equalling the semi-circle's radius. Vaulting an oblong is not possible with semi-circular arches because the two arches on the shorter sides will be smaller and shorter than the arches on the longer sides. This means that Norman builders were only able to vault a square, for example a crossing tower. It also means that in order for the roof to be level, the width of a Norman nave had to be equal to the distance between the columns of the arcade.

If, however, the arches bridging the shorter sides of an oblong are squeezed out of shape until they reach up to a point of equal height with the two taller, semi-circular arches, the height of all four arches will be the same. Vaulting an oblong is one key virtue of the Gothic pointed arch. A pointed arch can withstand more pressure from above than a semi-circular arch, and it is able to support more weight. The weight will be exerted on the two places where it stands, and these places can in turn be supported by a BUTTRESS outside the building; the extra support means that thinner, less massive walls can be built. Where walls are less massive, windows can be safely introduced, so, from the thirteenth century, more and more of them appeared in churches. (A row of windows above the nave arcade is called a CLERESTORY, because of the *clarity* afforded by the light.) There is usually a regular rhythm of buttresses and bays – the spaces between buttresses – and this rhythm defines the elevation of a Gothic church.

It is also essential to understand the RIB VAULT, a very early example of which can be seen in the chancel aisle of Durham Cathedral (1104). Where two barrel vaults meet at right angles, the joints are called GROINS – lines of pressure easily visible from below. The principal RIBS in a vault follow the groins, concealing them. Transverse ribs run straight across from one side to the other, while diagonal ribs run across diagonally; they meet at the ridge of the vault. In a vaulted bay with two transverse ribs and two diagonal ribs, the space between the ribs will be in four parts (quadripartite). This area, which does not bear any weight, is called the 'web' and it may be filled by much lighter material than is used in a barrel vault. In later church architecture, the vaulting is yet more elaborate.

The rib vault is the skeleton that supports the roof, in the same way that a ridge tent has rigid poles supporting malleable canvas. In constructing a rib vault, the ribs are erected first, meeting in the middle at the ridge of the pointed roof. The meeting point is often concealed by a boss, which provides a significant focus for decoration. In the cloisters at Norwich Cathedral (1145), bosses are composed of wreaths and leaves, perhaps oak sheltering a squirrel, or the much favoured Green Man, a FROND-FEATURED FOREST SPIRIT and powerful pagan survivor in a muscular Christian age.

VESICA WINDOW

CINQUEFOIL

BLIND WINDOW

CLUSTER SHAFTS
I·E· COLUMN made up of smaller components

g-TOOTH

his heavy
collar
typical EE.

BINHAM PRIORY · NORFOLK – BECAME
PARISH CHURCH (MUCH REDUCED) AT REFORMATION
BUILT 1220-1240

ST ANDREW'S
BARNWELL
NORTHAMPTONSHIRE

QUATREFOIL

V. TYPICAL E·E
DOORWAY COMPOSED OF
SEVERAL CONCENTRIC
ORDERS

BLANK
QUATREFOILS

PETER'S RAUNDS · NORTHAMPTONSHIRE

GABLE

HALF
GABLE

STRING
COURSE

ST GEORGE'S · KENCOT · OXFORDSHIRE

THESE ARE BOTH PLATE
TRACERY The LOWER ONE
IS ALMOST BAR TRACERY
AS THE PASTRY-CUT LOOK IS REFINED

TRIPARTITE WINDOW WITH TREFO
HEAD

INTERSECTING Y-TRACERY

CLUSTERED
SHAFTS

BLIND ARCH

BALL-FLOWER   DOG-TOOTH   FRET

ST ANDREW'S
COTTERSTOCK
NORTHAMPTONSHIRE

STYLISED E/E

1400 CARVED REREDOS · ST MARY'S · BAMPTON · OXFORDSHIRE
FIGURES OF CHRIST & APOSTLES UNDER CROCKETTED GABLES

TRUMPET MOULDING

STIFF-LEAVED
CAPITAL

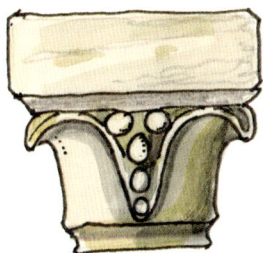

VARIOUS E/E CAPITALS

FONT

SCALLOPED
FRIEZE

COLONNETTES

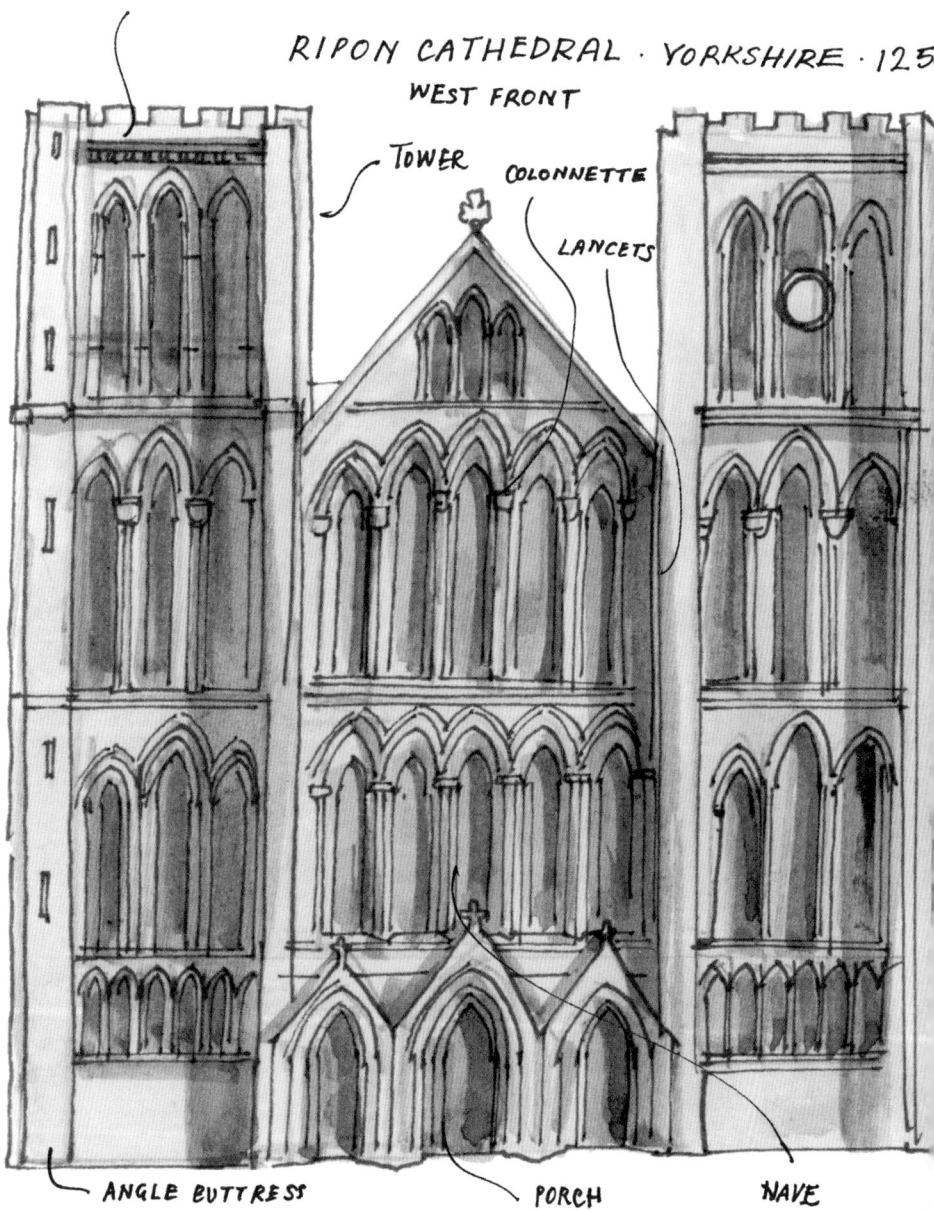

BATTLEMENT

RIPON CATHEDRAL · YORKSHIRE · 125
WEST FRONT

TOWER

COLONNETTE

LANCETS

ANGLE BUTTRESS

PORCH

NAVE

ST MARY'S
WEST WALTON
NORFOLK

FREE-STANDING
TOWER APART
FROM THE
CHURCH

PARAPET &
PINNACLES
ARE
PERP. MUCH
LATER

SHAFT

POLYGONAL
BUTTRESS

NAIL-HEAD
+ DOG-TOOTH

TALL
ARCADING

ARCHED
GABLE
NICHES
WITH
SHAFTS

TOWER IS
OPEN at
GROUND FLOOR
ON ALL
SIDES

61

DECORATED

Strange that the fourteenth century, a period of extreme VIOLENCE, DEATH, BATTLE AND HORROR, should have produced the Decorated style. In 1314, in a rare reversal of Scotland's usual fate against the English, the Scots led by Robert the Bruce defeated Edward II at Bannockburn most bloodily and decisively, destroying the flower of English chivalry. After that, Edward III carried his army across the Channel and used his terrifyingly powerful and highly trained long-bowmen to demolish the French in the 1346 Battle of Crécy, the first major battle on land in the Hundred Years War. However, it was another terrible attack, this time from the mysterious East, that really brought European society to a sudden halt. This was the Black Death, and by 1350 it had reduced the number of Edward III's subjects from four million to two and a half million souls, emptying villages and towns, putting up wages and changing the INERT FEUDALISM of early medieval Britain for ever.

Meanwhile, the English builders, still enthused with the architecture of France, moved into an efflorescent new building phase. While in France the FLAMBOYANT style carried the day, in England the DECORATED style, just slightly more modest and geometrical, was the language invented to counter all this darkness and despair. It was a dashing leap away from the austere rolls and lancets of the Early English approach.

As architectural aspiration led to the building of taller, slenderer churches and soaring towers, so buttresses needed to reach higher and wider, until they became the flying buttresses you can see at Bath Abbey and the cathedrals of Salisbury, Chichester and Canterbury. In England, buttresses were gently and artfully stepped to the ground in three or four removes. In order to increase stability, they were surmounted by crocketted gables, fashioned into finials and spirelets, as at Dronfield in Derbyshire (c.1300). Buttresses might also be embellished with niches for statuary.

With the explosion of decoration came a new language of ornament: fleuron and ball-flower adorned niche and tomb, chantry chapel and porch, reredos and pew, choir stall and font, and pulpit. After the crisp refinement of Early English style, the simplicity of the formula for designing churches was challenged as erect architectural lines began to stray into the Decorated style.

Southwell Minster in Nottinghamshire is a good place to appreciate the form that this straying may take. It is also a stonking church in its own right. In its Chapter House (1290) the capitals are at eye level and are carved exquisitely with leaves drawn from the English countryside. These leaves so envelop each capital that the bell shape beneath is only just visible. More than that, the leaves, which began as mere clothing for the capitals, seem to have secured roots of their own, reaching outside their proper bounds. They creep, here and there, beyond the capital, along the lintel or up the side of a springing arch, as if they are spreading almost uncontrollably.

Inside Southwell Minster, the gables of the stone rood screen are luxuriously crocketted. They also display crocketted sedilia, flying ribs and diaper patterning. This is all worth travelling a long way to see, but what is quintessentially Decorated here is the shape of the rood screen's gables: the basic lancet form has been manipulated into an experimental, highly ornamented S-shape – an ogee.

The most overwhelming example of the exotic ogee form is in the rectangular Lady Chapel of Ely Cathedral (about 1335). Allow for the terrible damage caused by outraged iconoclasts and Puritans, and the lack of colour that once adorned the chapel, and observe how what could be a severe line of seating is instead a series of niches, covered as they are by canopies of nodding ogee arches that wave and undulate around the room. These ogee arches, standing proud of the wall, are cusped and crocketted.

This English joy in – and genius for – decoration is combined with an appreciation of how the enclosure of space works. After the Norman crossing tower at Ely collapsed in 1322, plans were laid for an octagonal replacement. Known as a lantern, the eight windows which now rise above the bounds of the roof pour light into the space below, to take anyone proceeding eastward along the nave by surprise and fill them with joy. Fashioned by master-carpenter William Hurley, the structure is an exemplar of the EXTRAORDINARY INGENUITY of fourteenth-century woodwork. This astonishing space is a prime achievement to emerge from the Decorated period. Further east, the chancel vault (1335) displays a procession of liernes making lively dodecagonal patterns.

Seen from the King's Lynn train across the water meadows, the cathedral stands on what was once an island in the Cambridgeshire washes. It is prominent amid a landscape so utterly flat and it rises to the heavens, crowned by the much-glazed lantern which cuts into the East Anglian skies. As the largest building within at least a day's travel when it was built, the cathedral was an impressive expression of SPIRITUAL and, indeed, WORLDLY POWER. It was also the realisation of new architectural forms and vocabulary, carved in stone and wood.

The energy that fourteenth-century builders put into creating new extensions of space and experimenting with line and shape can still be seen, and experienced, in Bristol. The medieval chancel of the cathedral (1298–1330) boasts unique and unexpected vistas and views that are angled on the diagonal. The weight of the chancel vault, which would normally have been carried by an external flying buttress running from the roof to the ground, is instead carried by a horizontal bridge within the interior of the church. This bridge stretches out below the aisle's transverse arches and ribs reach up from its centre to support the vault. Both arches and ribs are slender, and the webbing between them is partially omitted so that when the visitor looks upwards, their line of vision goes both along and diagonally, and they experience the whole chancel space at once. It was PRODIGIOUS ENGINEERING INNOVATION that allowed for – and contributed to – this most startling and subtle aesthetic expression.

The chancel vault is a further demonstration of skilled design. Liernes – ribs that have no structural role – draw attention to themselves by being cusped and placed to create lozenges running around the ridge, as far as the east window. Within the cathedral, you can closely study what is in effect a model for the use of ribs: in the tiny room leading to the Berkeley Chapel, the ceiling, only just above the head, is flat and yet it appears to be supported by arches, ribs and bosses. They are, in fact, entirely decorative. (A brief study of these is a useful lesson learned in the nomenclature of vault-making.)

Since 1300, towards the end of Edward I's reign, it seemed that decoration had come to be as important as structure. As every piece of structure in church design became lavishly embellished, that very embellishment became an end unto itself and, in turn, required new structures of its own to support it. This was particularly the case for the tracery of large windows.

Early English windows had used PLATE TRACERY, where the flat stone spandrel above a pair of lancets was pierced by a quatrefoil or roundel, and they had also employed BAR TRACERY, which was composed of stone mullions growing into a variety of shapes, often incorporating cusped circles. DECORATED brought in another thing altogether. Tracery became both cursive and complex, and a perfect new medium in which to express this most evolved of Gothic styles.

The Perpendicular style was yet to come, a final rehearsing of the Gothic theme which was to abandon the elaborate fancies of Decorated for a more rigid and repetitive language. Then, increasing the proportion of glass to stone would become more important than pattern.

With the introduction of the S-shape into tracery, the patterns began to flow into the flame-like shapes of daggers and mouchettes under ogival window heads; repeated ogees produced 'reticulated', net-like tracery; and windows became larger, allowing more room for the elaboration of these curvilinear patterns. The enthusiasm for decorating churches as lavishly as possible was widespread, and today there are countless surviving examples in every county. All Saints Hawton, Nottinghamshire (1330), has a window of seven Decorated lights, and St Wulfram's, Grantham, Lincolnshire (1350), has three fine windows in its south chapel, each with a varied form of tracery. There is Carlisle Cathedral; St Cassian's Chaddesley Corbett in Worcestershire; the cloister and its door at Norwich Cathedral... and thousands more.

In many ways, the Decorated style is what most people mean by GOTHIC. This was the style to be developed most fully and joyfully by revivalists in the nineteenth century. It is, in stone at least, the apogee of Gothic craftsmanship (the wood-carver takes over this mantle in the next phase). The contrived and convoluted returns, swoops and cusps are the epitome of Gothic, and it is the Decorated vocabulary that has been reworked around the world, whenever the intention was to reproduce the parish church of home under a tropical sun. Decorated features can also be seen, in various degrees of dilution, in every nineteenth-century suburban church in London and elsewhere.

GARGOYLE

THE PERFECT, SIMPLE, LONG CHANCEL WITH LARGE DECORATED
WINDOWS · St ANDREW'S · COTTERSTOCK · NORTHAMPTONSHIRE · 1337

STRING COURS

ST BOTOLPH'S, BOSTON, LINCOLNSHIRE
"THE BOSTON STUMP" 1309
(272' HIGH)

PARAPET

OCTAGONAL
LANTERN

BUTTRESSES

NE CUT STONE

ANGLE
BUTTRESSES

BASE COURSE

PANELLING

INTRICATELY CARVED DECORATED
PANELLING

DORCHE
ABBEY
OXFORD

FOLIATE CROCKETTIN

OGEE
TREFOIL

PISCINA

FINIALS
PINNACLE?

HANGING PYX
TO STORE
CONSECRATED HOST
OUT OF HARM'S WAY...

CINQUEFOIL
NICHES

SEDILIA & PISCINA

CROWN

HAUNC

SPRING

RETICULATED
TRACERY

BAR TRACERY

FLAMBOYANT
TRACERY

ST MARY'S · MORPETH
NORTHUMBERLAND
BEFORE 1377

ST ANDREW'S · SHIFNAL
SHROPSHIRE · 1300

FISH-SCALE
TRACERY

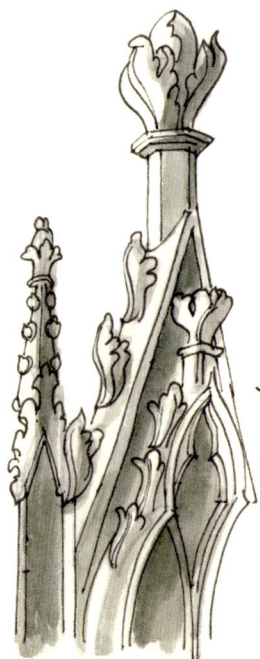

A NODDING
OGEE
NICHE

ST MARY & ALL SAINTS
WHALLEY · LANCASHIRE

RIPON CATHEDRAL

ST MICHAEL'S
MERE
WILTSHIRE

OGEE

QUOIN

SWOOPING OGEE

PINNACLE

CROCKETS ON PINNACLE

NICHE

FF ETS

DIAGONAL BUTTRESSES

ST MICHAEL'S MERE WILTSHIRE

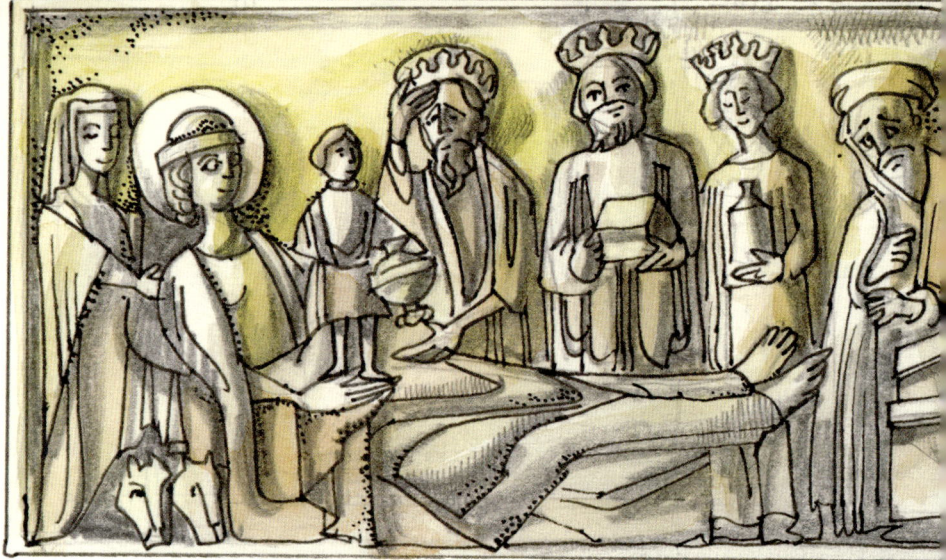

EARLY (14 ALABASTER
RELIEF
HOLY TRINITY
LONG MELFORD · SUFF[

ST FAITH'S
LITTLE WITCHINGHAM
NORFOLK

ST PETER
WITH THE
KEYS
OF ROME

PERPENDICULAR

The last phase of the Gothic movement established a peculiarly English style, one that would, many centuries later, vie with the architectural style of ancient Rome when Britain was deciding how to dress its new Houses of Parliament in 1840. In the fourteenth century, Englishness finally started to be clearly defined. Up until then, national identity and links with the Continent had continued hand in hand, in law and literature as well as in architecture: it was not until three hundred years after the French-Norman Conquest of 1066 that a statute was passed providing that pleadings in all courts of law should be in English not French (although, in fact, the proceedings would be recorded in Latin). Meanwhile, Geoffrey Chaucer chose to write his *Canterbury Tales* not in French or Latin, but in English, the VULGAR TONGUE.

The Perpendicular period, which crossed over with the end of Decorated, had a brutal start. By the middle of this era, the country had suffered one hundred years of foreign war, draining it of manpower and resources. The Black Death had struck for the first time in 1349, and its annual and ubiquitous return was an ongoing fear. The radical proto-Protestantism of JOHN WYCLIFFE'S LOLLARDRY and his translation of the Bible into English disturbed the established Church, as did the Peasants' inevitable Revolts, rebellion by Owen Glendower in Wales, and Harry Hotspur's defeat at Shrewsbury.

Less than a decade after the first visitation of the Black Death, however, renovation, restoration and modernisation of monasteries, cathedrals and parish churches was resumed. Continuity and expansion, completing the plans of a former generation, and building in the newest London style is what we see in this third period of Gothic architecture.

As its name suggests, Perpendicular relies on the repeated use of vertical members, particularly in glazing and wall panelling. This can seem almost ALARMINGLY SIMPLE when compared with the articulated and elaborate Decorated style with which it competed, and which it eventually superseded. (It would, of course, be simpler if the two styles were less cosily coeval, but there it is. Decorated runs from 1240 to 1360 and Perpendicular from 1335 to 1530.)

In fact, Perpendicular can be seen as a reaction against the flowing, curvilinear, ogival forms of Decorated. Decorated is a celebration of VARIETY, Perpendicular of UNIFORMITY. Where Decorated windows are varied to create richness, Perpendicular windows demonstrate dignified regularity. In Perpendicular window tracery, vertical mullions and horizontal transoms meet to create panels, doing away with the previous curly language of Decorated tracery. This, of course, is a boon to the glazier, as it allows the use of smaller panes. Rectangular mouldings surrounding windows and doorways contain spandrels; these curved triangles provide a new field for decoration and become the focus for great creativity in doorways and in panelling.

To understand the essence of the Perpendicular style, and, indeed, to see it in the context of the Decorated style, turn to the great mitred abbey of Gloucester. ('Mitred' because the head of a cathedral would wear a headdress called a mitre. After the abbey was dissolved by Henry VIII in the sixteenth century, he converted it into a cathedral.) It was originally a large Norman structure with an apsidal end. The nave's great cylindrical drum piers conjure the massiveness of Stonehenge; it is a formidable space. Then, further east, a great and important stylistic change occurs: from Norman comes Decorated, then Perpendicular.

It begins with the tomb of Edward II, which is a DEFINITIVE EXEMPLAR of Decorated style, completed in 1335. After the king's mutilated body had been rejected by several other abbeys for fear of reprisals from Isabella, Edward's widowed queen, and her lover Mortimer (who had together conspired for his downfall and death), it was received and buried here. The tomb is aedicular, which means it is a miniaturised version of a full-size architectural element – in this case, the tomb is a masterpiece complete with vaulting, ogees and crocketted finials. The making of the king's effigy was one of the earliest uses of alabaster and the result is both moving and expressive. The sad royal head, with SINUOUS TWISTING BEARD and hair, is supported by two blind-eyed, devoted angels. The tomb of this king, so hated when he was alive, is made of the finest grained oolitic limestone and Purbeck marble. It quickly became the focus of devoted and long-lived pilgrimage.

The Church received large sums of money from Edward III, as well as from pilgrims, and this allowed the whole eastern arm of the abbey to be re-clothed in the Perpendicular style. 'Re-clothed' because the Norman choir, with its deep gallery and triforium, was not pulled down to make way for its replacement. The newer choir THRUSTS UP SHAFTS to meet the traceried windows, masking the Norman piers. The Perpendicular renovation then descends, covering the walls with cusped panels and acting as a grille over the Norman arcade. This new dress is like a skeleton over the thick Norman walls.

The juxtaposition of Norman and late Gothic architecture in the chancel exaggerates the difference between them: Norman design has the appearance of being planned from the foundations upwards, whereas Gothic seems to pour down from the bosses, through the tracery of the clerestory windows and down the uninterrupted shafts. The choir leads towards a glass wall at the east end of the church. This truly astonishing canted window is built across the walls of the apse, which are deflected outwards. The mullions and transoms of the window meet to create tiers of panels, each with a full-length glass figure in white, blue, yellow and red. This Perpendicular, rectilinear treatment of the window and choir set the architectural scene for the next two hundred years.

But what is, perhaps, most immediately and easily recognisable in the Perpendicular style is fan vaulting. This, along with piercing (the hollowing out of battlements and parapets into filigree stone webs) is one area where Perpendicular means more decoration and not less. Its great examples are St George's Chapel, Windsor (1475), the Henry VII Chapel in Westminster Abbey (1503), and King's College Chapel in Cambridge (1446). It is startling, and unforgettable. A FAN VAULT has all the ribs curving from one springer, all the same length, all the same distance from the next, and all with the same curvature, containing panels between each pair like the folds of a fan.

The Henry VII Chapel in Westminster Abbey, for all that it is small, is overwhelming. Its elaborately ornamented fan vault is made all the more sumptuously excessive by its profusion of hanging PENDANTS. The vault rests upon polygonal turrets, visible from the outside, which bear panelling that echoes the alternating windows. There is a lavishness as well as lightness about the entire chapel.

At King's College Chapel in Cambridge, the fan vaults appear to balance on walls of glass. For vaulting that demonstrates uniformity, repetitive splendour and magnificence, nothing can compare with the showmanship of this. These rows of panelled clerestory windows, though filled with coloured instead of clear glass in some places, allow daylight and a sense of airiness to flow through the church. Although it is not the case here, Perpendicular CLERESTORIES were often supported by already existing Early English or Decorated arcades. Light is, indeed, the result of all that Perpendicular achieves.

The roof of a church is, in many instances, especially in East Anglia and Somerset, its most exciting element. Britain has traditionally been a timber-using country because of its naval history, and it has produced carpenters capable of designing roofs of ingenuity, variety and beauty.

A simple roof consists of rafters pitched against each other and meeting at the ridge. In a characteristic DEVON church, every rafter has curved braces, and the effect is like the canvas roof of a covered wagon, especially if the spaces between the timbers are plastered or 'ceiled'. If the roof is not ceiled, but open to the ridge, the whole structure is visible. Roofs became more complicated in the Perpendicular era, a series of collars and braces. These provided new fields for craftsmanship and design. There were chambers, battlements and hammers, frequently adorned with carved and gilded wooden angels.

This was a time of expansion, a period of church extension and reordering when roofs were renewed, as were chancels and even naves. Porches, often with rooms above, were rebuilt and churches were refenestrated, allowing light to flood into once-dark medieval interiors. There was formidable new building, as well as the completion of previously unfinished TOWERS, with some counties being manifestly more boastful than others. There are examples of towered Perpendicular churches in Lincolnshire, Cumbria and Cornwall, and in Gloucestershire there is the curious wooden tower of St Mary's in Upleadon (c.1500). Somerset has fine, distinctive designs that rise up in stages, as at St Michael's in Dundry, where the 1484 tower was once a beacon for sailors. In the east, the great Perpendicular WOOL CHURCHES of Norfolk and Suffolk soar into East Anglia's big skies; the churches at Long Melford (1484) and Blythburgh (1412) seem more glass than wall. In the Norfolk fens, that black-soiled prairie once all reeds and marsh, look for the church of Walpole St Peter (1425), whose austere Perpendicular design is a most elegant apogee of the last shout of Gothic style.

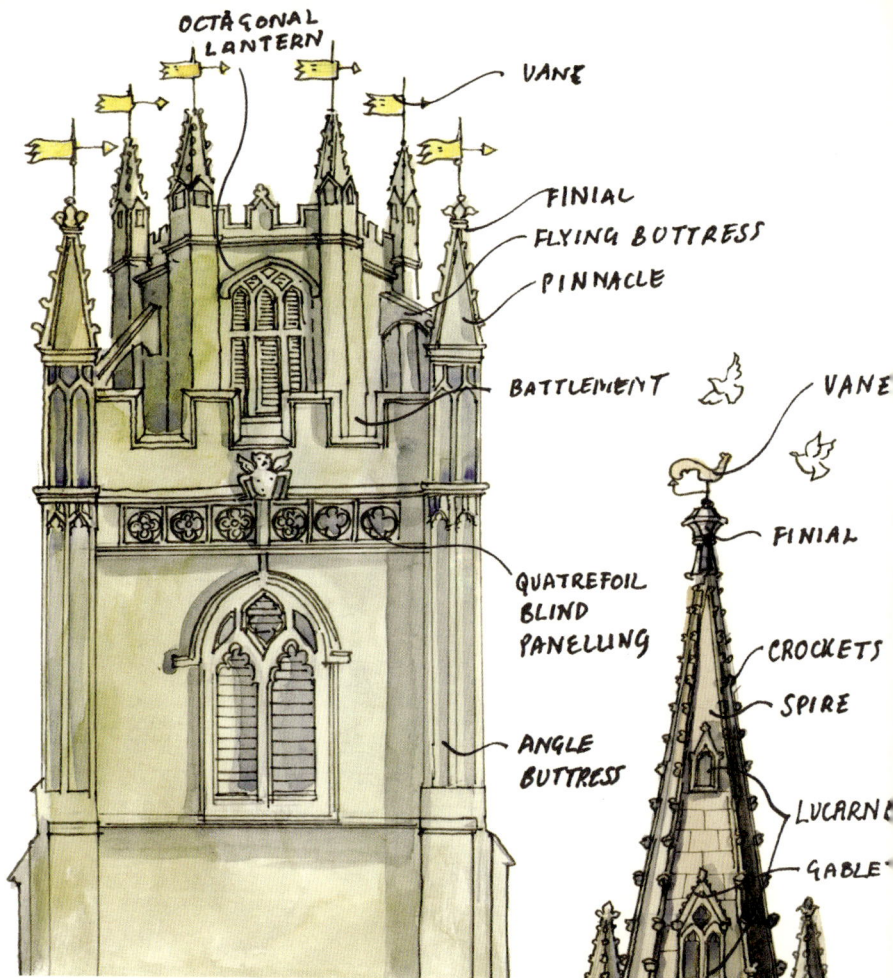

OCTAGONAL LANTERN

VANE

FINIAL

FLYING BUTTRESS

PINNACLE

BATTLEMENT

VANE

FINIAL

QUATREFOIL BLIND PANELLING

CROCKETS

SPIRE

LUCARNE

GABLE

ANGLE BUTTRESS

ST PETER'S · LOWICK NORTHAMPTONSHIRE

ANGLE PINNACLE

LANTERN

ST MARY & ALL SAINTS NASSINGTON NORHAMPTONSHIRE

MOULDED PLINTH

STAGE

PARAPET

PANELLING

WINDOWS WITH
SEGMENTAL
HEADS

MULLIONS

STEPPED BUTTRESS

The Blessed Virgin Mary

ROOD (The Cross)

Christ Crucified

JOHN the Baptist

Supporting ANGEL

GALLERY

COVING

VAULT

CROCKET

ARCADE

PAINTED PANELS

A ROOD SCREEN OF THE KIND SMASHED BY THE ICONOCLASTS OF THE REFORMATION & THE COMMONWEALTH IN THE ⑯ & ⑰. THIS DIVIDED THE CHANCEL FROM THE NAVE: THE SACRED FROM THE CIVIC & WAS A FOCUS FOR THE CONGREGATION AS THEY SAT IN DEVOTION. MANY, HOWEVER, HAVE BEEN SAVED OR WERE RESTORED IN THE ⑲. SOME RETAIN VIOLENT SCRATCH MARKS ACROSS SAINTS' FACES OR THE SYMBOLS OF THEIR MARTYRDOM, ANATHEMA TO REFORMING PROTESTANTS.

PERPENDICULAR 1335–1530   89

VERY TYPICAL PERPENDICULAR
DECORATION IN REPEATING
PANELS. SOPHISTICATED
& V. FINE CARVING

BLIND PANEL

BLIND-PANEL
TRACERY

OGEE

CRENEL MERLON

PANELLED
BATTLEMENT

ARCHIVOLT

OFF
SETS

OGEE
ARCH

ANGLE BUTTRESS

THREE CONCENTRIC
ARCHES

SEGMENTAL
ARCH

POINTED
ARCH

TREFOIL

WEST DOOR

ST NICHOLAS'S
KING'S LYNN
NORFOLK
1419

DOUBLE
HOODMOULD.
SO TWO
PAIRS OF
SPANDRELS

HEAD STOP

PANELLING

* This door was once
PAINTED

CINQUEFOIL

(FOUR-CENTRED ARCH
GETTING LESS
GOTHIC)

CUSPING

QUATREFOIL

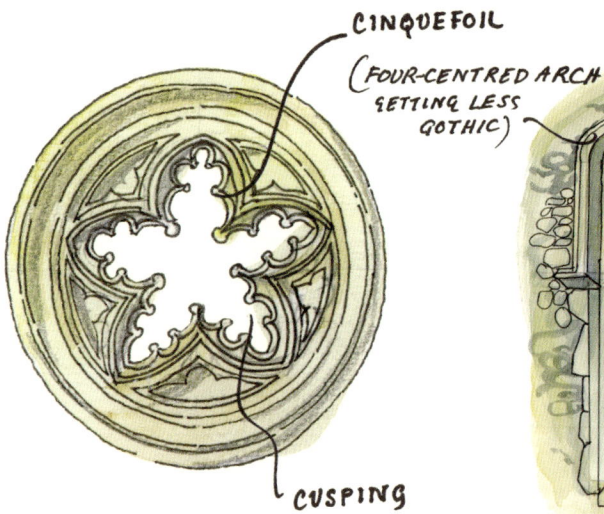

SO MUCH *GLASS*, THE
WINDOW TAKES UP MOST OF WEST
WALL

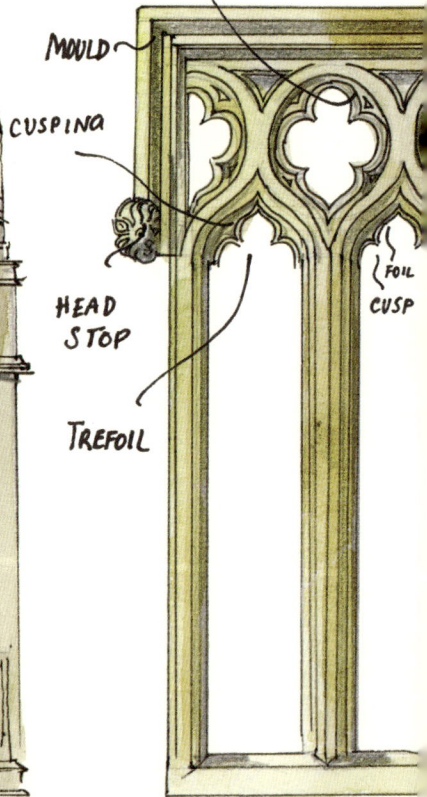

MOULD

CUSPING

HEAD
STOP

FOIL
CUSP

TREFOIL

ST MARY'S CHURCH. UFFINGTON

STRANGE
SIMPLE
MULLIONS
(CD be (17)

RINHAM PRIORY - The dissolved
priory Church's aisles are
destroyed and almost
"SECULAR" straight-topped
windows inserted in the arcade...

STILTED
HOOD
MOULD

(16) WINDOW

(13) AISLE ARCH

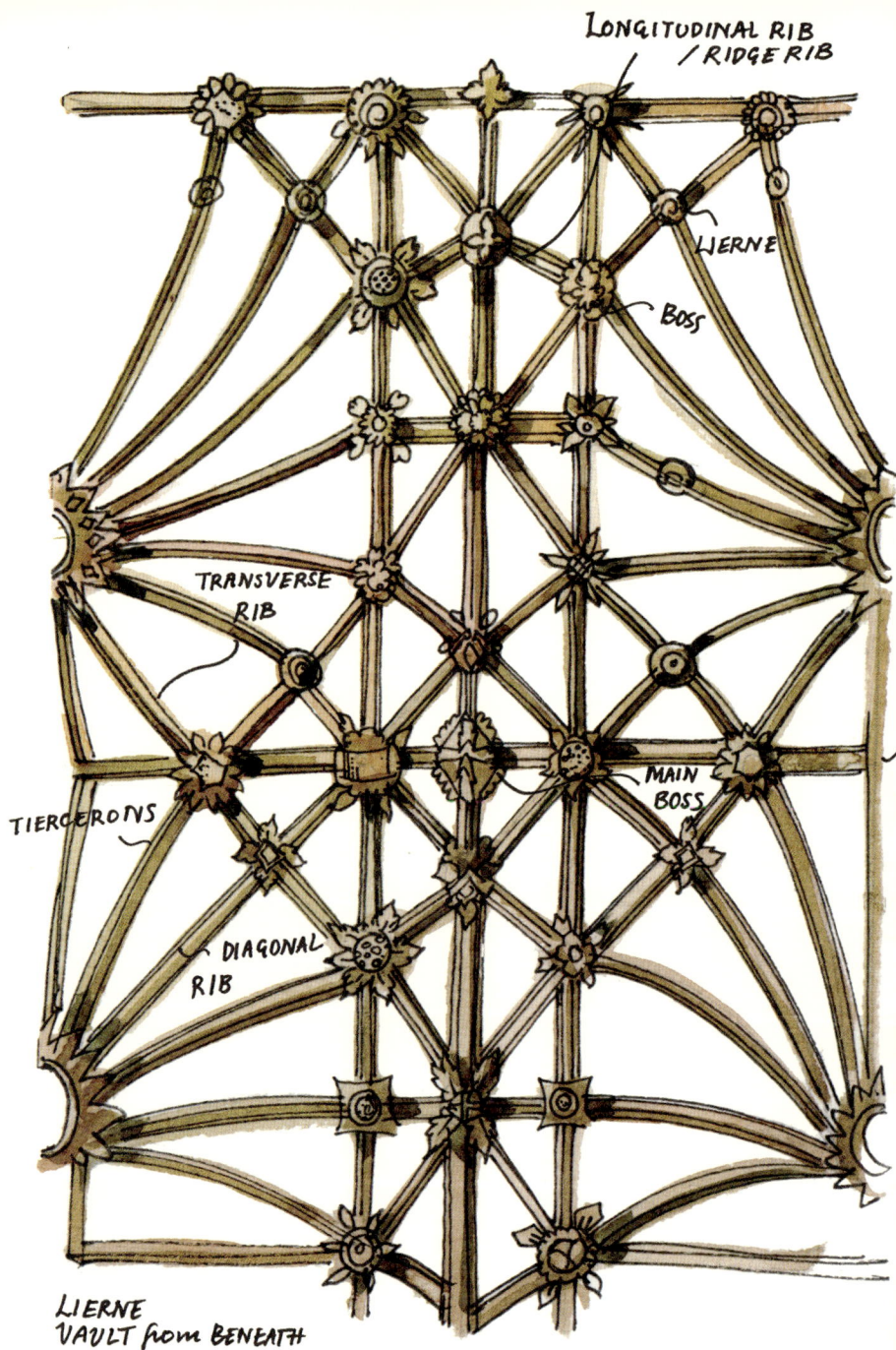

LONGITUDINAL RIB / RIDGE RIB

LIERNE

BOSS

TRANSVERSE RIB

TIERCERONS

MAIN BOSS

DIAGONAL RIB

LIERNE VAULT from BENEATH

SIMPLE PARAPET

DAGGER

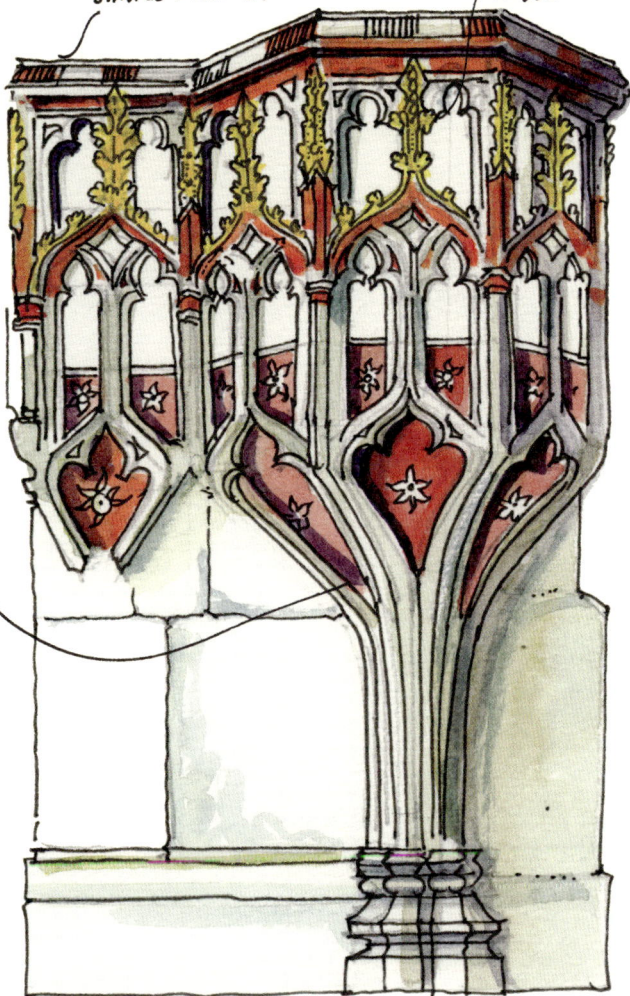

* A REMARKABLE
REFORMATION
SURVIVOR. PERHAPS
DUE TO ITS LACK OF
RELIGIOUS IMAGERY

RIB

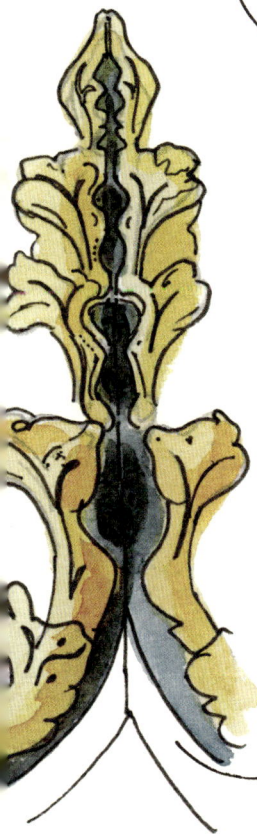

THIS PULPIT at ST JOHN The BAPTIST
CIRENCESTER, GLOUCESTERSHIRE IS (for obvious
reasons) CALLED A WINE-GLASS PULPIT
(15 . PAINTED & GILDED

DETAIL of CROCKETS ON
PINNACLE SHOWING their
FOLIATE FORM

LOVE THY GOD ALONE

BAROQUE & GOTHIC SURVIVAL

The reigns of Edward VI, Mary and Elizabeth I produced VERY FEW CHURCHES. If you find yourself today in a church built between 1537 and 1603, take good note of its origin, who built it and why. This is a backwater of church-building. It was in the old parish churches that people heard the Word and read from the newly sanctioned English translation of the Bible.

During the sixteenth century the Church, which had for so long developed slowly and organically, suffered a series of convulsions that left it SHAKEN AND ENFEEBLED right up until the nineteenth century. The Reformation and the Dissolution of the Monasteries marked the end of the Perpendicular style, and the total shock of the upheavals put church building projects on hold.

In 1534, Henry VIII, for a variety of reasons dynastic, economic, political and passionate, made his break from Rome. Thomas Cromwell, his chief minister, saw the riches of the Church as a sort of goldmine, one that would refill the exchequer that his expensive monarch had seriously depleted. He had no sentimentality whatsoever about what the parish church, its chantries and chapels, its images and its treasure meant to its local parishioners. As screens were lost, precious metals melted, wall paintings whitewashed and STATUARY DEFORMED, the interiors of parish churches and cathedrals alike were disordered or destroyed. Abbeys and priories were sold for stone, and the accreted works of five hundred years of Britain's best design and craftsmanship were turned overnight into mere quarries.

The outlawing and destruction of monasteries between 1536 and 1540 forced monks out into the world, but initially it had left parish church buildings untouched. Having finished with the monastic institutions, reform continued in the name of nine-year-old Edward VI, who acceded to the throne in 1547. Encouraged by the Protestantism of his uncle the Lord Protector, Duke of Somerset, reformers scoured the country for churches, systematically destroying chantry chapels, defacing wall paintings, beheading images, smashing saints portrayed in glass, and removing stone altars. They brought in simple wooden panels broadcasting the Lord's Prayer, Creed and Ten Commandments in bold black writing for the literate, in place of the rood for the superstitious.

The Protestant reforms were a top-down series of changes led by intellectual and political shifts at Court, not by a groundswell of dissatisfaction in the villages of Britain. Villagers must, then, have been elated half a dozen years later when Catholic Queen Mary countermanded these orders. Hasty replacement and refurbishing ensued, with woodwork, needlework, glass, treasures and images restored. The first wave of destruction had often been met by subterfuge; graven images had been hidden in barns or homes ready for their hoped-for return, thus facilitating Marian reforms. But it was not to last. The year 1558 brought the return of a Protestant monarch, Elizabeth I, and a strict prescriptive Prayer Book followed in 1559. The advent of this PURITANISM was to affect church interiors for three hundred years.

The new churchmanship, which continued under the rule of James I in the seventeenth century, meant renewed focus on the church interior. The Protestant emphasis on corporate worship, and the importance of hearing and understanding the hard-line sermons being preached, brought the officiating minister into the body of the church. PREACHING enjoyed a remarkable vogue. The minister required a pulpit from which to preach and his clerk a reading desk from which to lead the Amen. Jacobean pulpits are common today and are easily recognisable: usually unpainted oak, octagonal with carved panels, sometimes with a reader's desk attached for the parson to read the service from the lower deck and then mount to the upper deck to overlook box-pews or meet the galleries face to face. Occasionally, with the addition of a clerk's desk, a pulpit would become a three-decker; it might boast a tester above, a sounding board to improve acoustics.

At that time, the pulpit would often be placed obstructing the view of the wooden altar table; the altar, where the mysteries of the Roman Catholic Mass had been acted out in a FOG OF INCENSE and to a TINKLING OF BELLS, was marginalised completely. Pews were set to face the pulpit. Chantry chapels, where prayers for the dead, at their expense, had been offered in perpetuity, had already been forbidden by Henry VIII; the parclose screens that had protected them were repositioned to enclose family pews instead.

In 1627, the Queen's Chapel at St James's was built by the architect Inigo Jones. This was the first time that the word 'architect' had been used with reference to a church. He had been to Italy and closely studied, like no Englishman before him, the work of Andrea Palladio, whose *Quattro Libri dell'Architettura* became Jones's Classical ideal. The Queen's House, Greenwich, had risen in 1619, astonishing his contemporaries, followed by the King's Banqueting House, Whitehall, in 1622. Jones conceived a building as a whole, organised according to rules. In spite of the constant visits to the Continent by men of learning and the importing of Classical details from France and Italy, not until Jones had anyone in England perfectly understood the essence of the architectural Renaissance revealed by Palladio. In 1631, Jones designed St Paul's, Covent Garden; constructed in 1633, it was the first completely new church built in London since the Reformation. Such sophisticated, assured Classicism had never before been seen in one of the capital's churches.

Matthew Wren, Master of the Cambridge college Peterhouse, introduced a chapel there in 1632, building on the style of Jones's Queen's Chapel. A hybrid of captivating charm, this is a totally transitional building, a stone-built expression of the revolution from Gothic to Classical that was changing European architecture. From the street, one sees a Perpendicular east window, but it sits beneath a Classical pedimented gable. This contrasts again with the decidedly un-Classical Flemish gable at the west. In 1662, when he was Bishop of Ely, Wren licensed the college chapel at Pembroke. But it was another Wren, Christopher, who designed it. One hundred yards away, on the same street, Pembroke challenges Peterhouse: its chapel is the first in either Oxford or Cambridge to be completely void of GOTHIC FEATURES. To the west, it has a round-topped window, four Corinthian pilasters and a pediment with an octagonal lantern. The stylistic battle is over, Gothic vanquished.

In between, there had been the Civil Wars of 1642 to 1649. From then until 1660, Britain was ruled by Oliver Cromwell, the Lord Protector. During the Puritans' (relatively brief) ascendancy over Royalists, a period of political and religious uncertainty, church-building was, unsurprisingly, suspended. To build a church could be construed as tantamount to an act of defiance, as the established architectural styles inevitably harked back to earlier, more elaborate and mysterious days. It was impossible to build securely during the Commonwealth and much that had been built was once again destroyed during that PERIOD OF ICONOCLASM.

With the restoration of Charles II in 1660 came the arrival of the Baroque style and a new Golden Age in church-building, particularly in the capital. London's burgeoning population meant that the city had many small parishes, and a staggering eighty-eight churches were consumed by flames during the Great Fire of 1666. This loss provided a broad new canvas for the genius of the age, Christopher Wren. He was a towering polymath; an inventor, mathematician, and professor of astronomy in London and at Oxford. Inspired by visits to France in 1665, he turned to architecture. He became King's Surveyor of Work in 1669 and, in 1670 alone, he designed seventeen new churches. Inigo Jones, instigator of British Classicism, had never had the opportunities that the Great Fire gave Wren.

Wren produced design variety through experimentation, solving the problems thrown up by cramped irregular sites or sloping ground, and, in broader terms, for meeting the needs of Anglican liturgies; there was no precedent for this in recent church architecture. It was obvious that light was important for observing ritual and for reading, and that congregations must be able to hear: a centralised or squared space seemed called for. For style, Wren had known and admired Jones's Roman-inspired work at St Paul's, Covent Garden, with its scrolls, octagonal lanterns, and obelisks as pinnacles. Among his twenty-three remaining churches, St Stephen Walbrook is a good place to discover the break from the medieval tradition. Money provided by the Grocers' Company, a medieval-style trade guild, meant expense was no barrier. Standing beneath the dome, which is carried on eight equal arches, are a nave, chancel and transepts. From this apparently traditional cruciform ground plan, Wren had produced a centrally planned auditory chamber exactly suited to the needs of the new Anglican Church.

The furniture and fittings for Wren's churches were generally paid for by the parish, but often to designs approved by the architect. Working with Wren were the amazing carver Grinling Gibbons, the painter Sir James Thornhill, and the finest maker of wrought-iron screens and gates, Jean Tijou. When Wren's new St Paul's Cathedral was completed in 1700, hostile contemporaries claimed that it was foreign and derivative. But to others, and to many of us today, Wren's interpretation of Classicism, with its raised Italian dome, has a uniquely commanding power.

PARAPET

CORNICE

ST ANDREW BY
The WARDROBE LONDON
built by Christopher
Wren in 1695 two
years before the first
service was celebrated
in nearby St Paul's
Cathedral.

BELL CHAMBER

PILASTER

PLAIT BAND

LOBED ARCHITRAVE

QUOINS

✻ THE WHOLE LANGUAGE OF CHURCH
ARCHITECTURE HAS CHANGED from
GOTHIC to CLASSICAL

BUTTRESSES TO PILASTERS - HOOD
MOULDS TO ARCHITRAVES - CORBEL
TABLES TO CORNICES and PINNACLES
TO URNS · THIS IS REVOLUTION not
EVOLUTION...

CORNICE WITH DENTILS

... & THE LANGUAGE IS DIFFERENT INSIDE AS WELL. This Screen has no Vaults or CROCKETS only CAPITALS and RENAISSANCE DECORATIVE ELEMENTS

EARLY C17 STYLE ~ JACOBEAN NOT BAROQUE

PEDIMENT

FLUTED
PILASTER

WALPOLE ST PETER'S NORFOLK
(17) SCREEN (POSS 1670)

OPEN BALUSTRADING

DADO

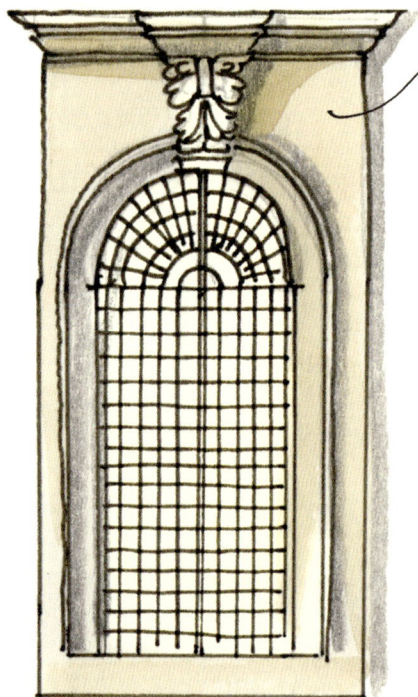

KEYSTON[E]

VOUSS[OIR]

SILL

KEYSTONE

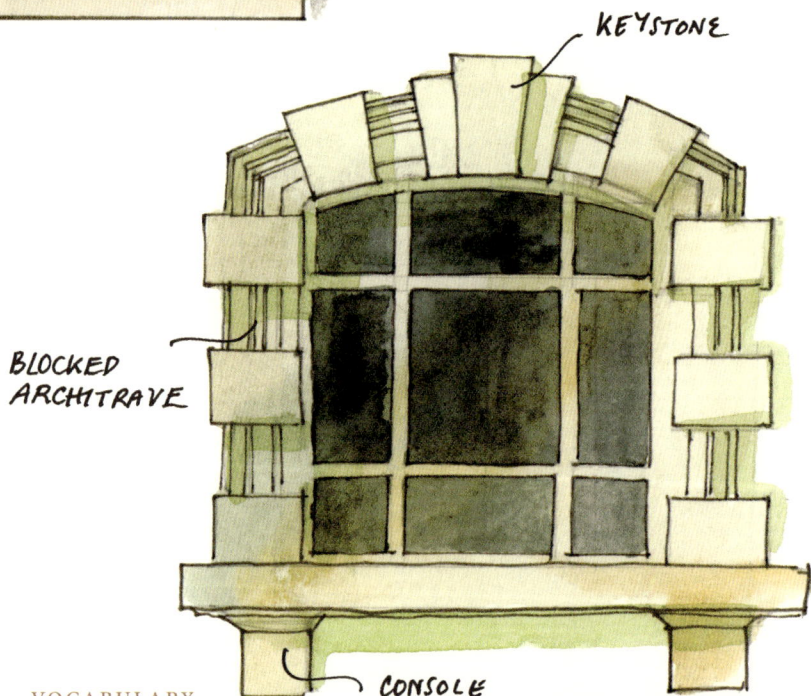

BLOCKED
ARCHITRAVE

CONSOLE

FRIEZE

BROKEN
PEDIMENT

FESTOON

SCROLL

FLUTED PILASTER

ST LAWRENCE JEWRY
LONDON

ST PAUL'S, COVENT GARDEN · INIGO JONES
1633 · This PERFECT PALLADIAN TEMPLE
comes STRAIGHT from ITALY and the ANCIENTS.
AND It was built only 30 years after the
DEATH of ELIZABETH, last of the TUDORS. This
is COMPLETE MODERNITY

PROJECTING
PEDIMENT

TYMPANUM

DENTIL

V.
DEEP!

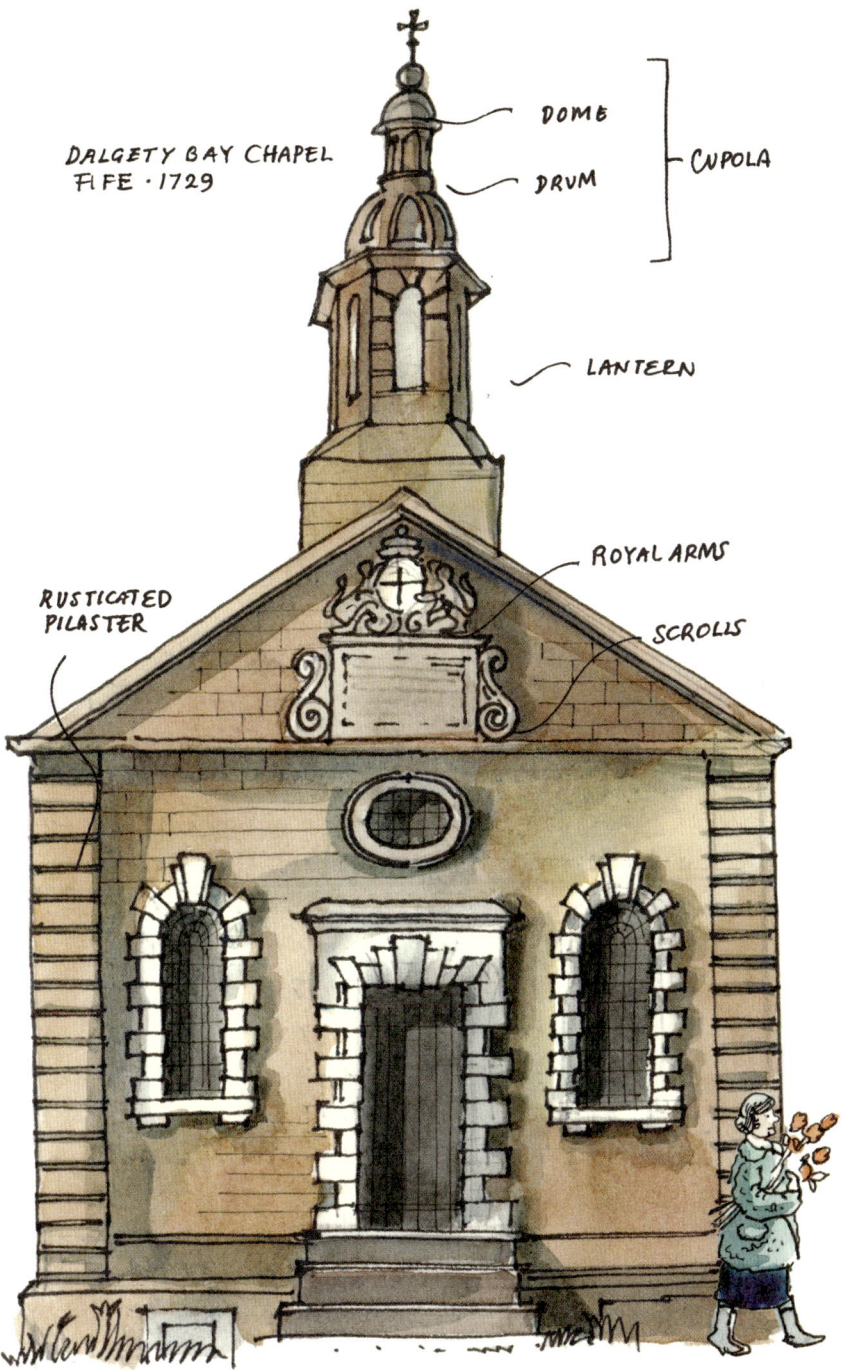

DALGETY BAY CHAPEL
FIFE · 1729

DOME

DRUM

CUPOLA

LANTERN

ROYAL ARMS

SCROLLS

RUSTICATED
PILASTER

WALPOLE OLD
CHAPEL · SUFFOLK · Converted
from Farmhouse in 1689 - Galleried Interior...

RIDGE

QUOINS   PLAIT BAND   LOBED ARCHITRAVE

FRIENDS MEETING HOUSE · JORDANS · BUCKINGHAMSHIRE
(Wm PENN, PROMINENT QUAKER FOR WHOM PENNSYLVANIA WAS
NAMED IS BURIED
HERE)

HIPPED
ROOF

CORNICE

THE OLD MEETING HOUSE · COLEGATE · NORWICH · 1693

ST MARY WOOLNOTH
CITY OF LONDON
(NICHOLAS HAWKSMOOR)
1716

ST GEORGE'S
BLOOMSBURY
LONDON
(NICHOLAS
HAWKSMOOR)
1731

RUSTICATION

ST MARY'S INGESTRE
STAFFORDSHIRE
(POSS CHRISTOPHER WREN)
1676

CHRIST CHURCH
SPITALFIELDS
LONDON
(NICHOLAS HAWKSMOOR)
1729

113

GEORGIAN

George I succeeded Queen Anne as British monarch in 1714 and, with his sons, gave his name to the Georgian period, which runs until his great-grandson William IV's death in 1837. This was the Age of Enlightenment. Religious tolerance and liberty under the law were envied abroad and prized at home. Roads were newly turnpiked, Improvement Acts ameliorated conditions in growing towns, Land was Enclosed. A feeling for display, a move from vernacular to urbane architectural expression, was practised and applauded.

The GRAND TOUR formed the most important part of the education of any gentleman already well versed in Latin and Greek. Great victories over the French in the War of the Spanish Succession had been won by the Duke of Marlborough and these were followed by the Treaty of Utrecht in 1713. This brought peace to the Continent, opening it once more to British Grand Tourists who already had an unreasonable degree of self-confidence and national pride. They would visit Paris and Rome and Venice to be civilised. They would discover the work of Vitruvius, architect and theorist of the ancient world, and be rowed down the Brenta canal which runs by so many of Palladio's villas. On their return home, they would learn to admire Inigo Jones, who had been largely responsible for introducing the Classical Palladian style into Jacobean England.

Inigo Jones, Palladio and Vitruvius – the seventeenth-century Englishman, the sixteenth-century Italian and the ancient Roman – were the guiding lights of the architectural revolution that the Earl of Burlington now accomplished with his associates Colen Campbell and William Kent.

Campbell brought out his first volume of *Vitruvius Britannicus* in 1715. It is a collection of large engravings of British buildings from the seventeenth and eighteenth centuries. The preface proclaims the SUPREME VIRTUES OF ANTIQUE SIMPLICITY, contrasting it critically with Christopher Wren's affected and licentious Baroque. The eighteenth century is the era of Protestantism, but, even so, there was a continuous fear of foreign, specifically French, Catholicism creeping in. Thus the architects of this Georgian period, full of self-esteem, the cloak of Classical Rome fitting neatly on their shoulders, picked up where Jones left off and built an Arcadian world. The COUNTRY HOUSE and the LANDSCAPE PARK were England's great cultural gifts to the world. This is where our architectural genius was concentrated. In terms of churches, these Palladians contributed little, although their influence was powerful.

The Palladian-Roman style felt too uncomfortably Roman Catholic to make an easy transition into church architecture; nevertheless, the variety of Georgian churches is greater than might be supposed, particularly in their interiors. Necessary items at this time were the altar, rails, pulpit, desk, pews, font, and Commandment boards with the Lord's Prayer and royal coats of arms. An altarpiece was not essential, but often desirable. The pulpit and reading desk had traditionally been situated at the point where sacred space (chancel) and more secular (nave) met, symbolically ideal for interpreting the scriptures to the congregation. But this began to change; now the pulpit might be in the middle of one side, or even at the west end. At Teigh, Rutland (1789), it stands high over the west door; what is equally unusual is that the pews are set transverse, as in a college, facing each other across the nave and, more than this, that the walls are pink and the ceiling blue like a drawing room.

The typical Georgian nave, which had box-pews with doors, looked almost domestic. Larger pews sometimes had a fireplace, a comfort denied to lower-status members of the congregation. Private family pews were sometimes in the transept, which had at times been purpose-built with a private entrance for the patron; from within the high-status pews, only the pulpit was visible.

One of the defining features of the eighteenth-century church was the gallery, a first floor inserted into the aisles and west end of a church. This was sometimes used as a minstrels' gallery, as is sweetly described in Thomas Hardy's *Under the Greenwood Tree.* But there were other galleries too: charity children sat in the north gallery; there were school and singing galleries; lofts or galleries for young persons to sit in and sing psalms; a gallery for menservants, and another for maidservants.

The chancel, seemingly empty apart from memorial tablets, was locked behind the chancel screen, illustrating how low the Eucharist had fallen in significance. Most walls were whitewashed, concealing any unsightly medieval or post-Reformation painting still remaining from an unfashionable past.

Royal coats of arms would be emblazoned over the chancel arch, replacing the old Catholic rood or rood screen. This dominance of secular over spiritual power is symbolic of the age. It was the time of the rise of the Assembly Rooms; they were the first secular public spaces built and were architecturally indistinguishable from their ecclesiastical contemporaries. In churches, the variation and elaborate artistry of arms and hatchments – armorial representation of church patrons – stress the Church's submission to the State and the gentry. Roofs were ceiled for warmth and, in keeping with the age, frequently decorated with Classical or Rococo plasterwork, making a drawing room of the house of God. Decoration reaches its zenith in Great Witley Church, Worcestershire (1735), where behind the Classical exterior, gilding gleams from every inch of the ornate plasterwork. Framing Antonio Bellucci's ceiling paintings, it is a LAST GASP OF BAROQUE SPLENDOUR.

Literacy was widespread, so pictures were by and large redundant. The Lord's Prayer and the Ten Commandments could be read on boards hanging either side of the altar. Candles were lit in brass sconces. Sometimes, expensive Dutch candelabras lit the nave, although it was still daylight when Evensong was sung in the early afternoon. Because this was an age when every man arrived wearing a hat, there were pegs lining the walls. From the reading desk in the lowest storey of the three-decker pulpit, the parish clerk would lead the way with the Amen and the congregation would repeat after him. An hourglass would hang by the pulpit. The nave seemed like a theatre – another new eighteenth-century building, as seen in Bury St Edmunds, Bath, and Richmond, Yorkshire – but it was one in which spectacle was pared down and monochrome.

Nuneham Courtenay, Oxfordshire, illustrates the social order of the eighteenth century in finely cut ashlar. In 1760, the old village and church were demolished by the 1st Earl Harcourt, who, in 1764, built All Saints Church in his park to designs from James 'Athenian' Stuart. Stuart had travelled to the dangerous Ottoman-held Athens with his co-author Nicholas Revett and the result of this was the publication of the first reliable sourcebook of Greek architecture, *Antiquities of Athens* (1762). All Saints is principally a landscape ornament with a pedimented Ionic portico; its Picturesque setting was more important to its patron than the convenience of the now-distant villagers who had to walk a mile across Lord Harcourt's park to say their prayers.

'Let sleeping dogs lie' was satisfactory in many departments of national politics, but the Church of England's torpid attitude was shaken up by the vitality of the METHODISTS. By 1760, Methodism was the most highly coordinated and dynamic body of opinion in the country – in stark contrast to the Church of England, which was compromised by pluralism and which enjoyed tithes, sinecures and lay patronage. It was customary for Church of England vicars or rectors to reap the benefits of two or more parishes by installing a poor curate as their representative in the secondary ones where they were not themselves based. The curate would be left to administer what pastoral care he could. Methodism attacked the spiritual apathy that these vested interests could promote with its revolutionary perception of human relationships and the place of religion in society.

Like the Anglo-Saxon missionaries of centuries before, the Methodist John Wesley was driven to preaching in the fields, and to thousands. Significantly, the enthusiasm that fuelled the growth of Wesleyanism was in the hearts of non-radicals; this was not an anti-establishment movement, but an attempt at serious-minded reform. Part of the attraction of Methodism was that it not only held out the assurance of redemption to men of modest birth and education, but permitted them to offer the same enthusiastic assurance to others. From the industrial North to isolated rural communities, followers of Wesley built their chapels, all in Classical garb, restrained and austere, some nearly identical to Quaker meeting houses.

Initially, Methodism operated within the established Church but, by 1784, it had been rejected and had broken away entirely. By this time, in the space of twenty-five years, the enthusiastic thousands who followed Methodist preaching had built 356 chapels, often in places where there was no church. Nonconformist building was not limited to the Methodists; Baptists of varying types – Unitarians, Evangelists and Congregationalists – all colonised Britain's towns and villages. The simple three-bay, two-storey preaching-box became an omnipresent feature in England's landscape.

Perhaps this period, together with its predecessor, can be seen as a CLASSICAL BLIP IN THE GOTHIC TRADITION of church-building. But the great London churches, the Nonconformist cathedrals of the North, and their unobtrusive but elegant cousins elsewhere, all play their part in the history of British churches.

SHALLOW
DOME

DRUM

ALL SAINTS. NUNEHAM COURTENAY
OXFORDSHIRE
(JAMES "ATHENIAN" STUART) · 1764

DIOCLETIAN
WINDOW

ST JOHN'S
HACKNEY
LONDON

ALL SAINTS. NUNEHAM COURTENAY

ST EDMUND'S · WARKTON · NORTHAMPTONSHIRE

VENETIAN or
SERLIAN WINDOW

HATCHMENT

IN CŒLO QVIES

SHELTER FOR PREACHING OUTDOORS (EG AT GRAVESIDE)

CHANDELIER

JUG

FLAGON

CHALICE

ST LEONARD'S
SHOREDITCH
LONDON

REGENCY &
EARLY VICTORIAN

In 1818, with Napoleonic France now satisfactorily defeated, the lack of churches in the expanding suburbs of Britain became a matter of concern. There had been a massive move from the country to the city, and to the newly industrialised towns of the North of England. In that year, it was estimated that the population exceeded by two and a half million the available seating in the buildings of the Church of England. Meanwhile, the Church faced competition from the chapels of Nonconformists, whose popularity was on the rise, as well as from the recently emancipated Roman Catholics. So Parliament passed a Church Building Act, which established a new Commission to deal with this problem. The Commissioners' churches were built in order to provide education and spiritual benefits, and not the expensive grandeur of churches built a hundred years before.

The rapid building programme that ensued was felt by the government to be a way of stemming the risk of POPULAR GODLESS MOB VIOLENCE. Each church had to represent the most economical accommodation for the greatest number of people within the range of a preacher's voice, and one half of the seats were to be free for the poor. This would help the Church bring the working classes salvation from atheism and revolution.

The new churches were often based on designs by highly polished architects John Nash, John Soane and Charles Barry; they were not designed by Ecclesiological architects, a breed that was about to spring into existence. Commissioners' churches were to have a long, high nave, small chancel, spacious interiors, galleries supported by slender piers, buttresses and a west tower. The pulpit should not intercept a view of the altar, but all seats should be placed to face the preacher. These requirements allowed, but did not require, Gothic dress for churches. The same prescription could equally be delivered in formal Grecian attire, as at St Peter's, Chiswick (1827) or St George's in Eaton Square, London (1827). This developed into a full-blooded BATTLE OF STYLES.

Gothic was in the air. St Luke's in Chelsea, London (1819), was a fine and admired opening salvo for the Gothic style at a time when Romanticism from Germany had begun to infiltrate both philosophy and art. Guide books for the Lake District were followed by the lyrical ballads introducing, with a manifesto, the Romantic Lakeland poetry of Wordsworth and Coleridge. Even more influential, perhaps, was the novelist Sir Walter Scott who, after the terrors of the 1745 Scottish Rebellion, rendered the Highlands sentimentally tame. This invited a new curiosity about medieval culture that was inextricably associated with Gothic Romanticism, which had initally been a literary construct. A vogue for the Picturesque drew attention back to the austere remains of Britain's monasteries, crumbling for 250 years since the Dissolution in the 1530s. They were landscaped. They stood in lawns as if designed for the purpose. Amongst the increasingly travelling middle-class population, who were charmed by the beauty and variety of monastic ruins, there was soon a growing reaction against the RECTANGULAR PREACHING BOXES of the Commissioners' churches in favour of something more beautiful, and more suited to old Church ritual.

Enthusiasm had not previously been part of the Church of England, which traditionally dreaded spiritual excitement and display. But enthusiasm was elbowing its way in and was being embraced. A political faction called Young England devoted itself to almsgiving and to help and education for the poor. It encouraged priests to remain resident in their own parishes. Along with Catholic-influenced student groups of the Oxford Movement (which also had its roots in Cambridge), its members were known as Ecclesiologists. Meanwhile, the Clapham Sect, which included the anti-slavery campaigner William Wilberforce, fought for ideals of piety, morality and social action. This found an architectural manifestation in the more profound Gothicising of church-building, and a final rejection of the Classical, which was not to reappear for decades.

The Gothic Revivalist movement found its modest heroic proponent in the form of Augustus Welby Northmoor Pugin. During his short but extraordinarily active life, Pugin persuaded the English masters of taste that Gothic was, for ecclesiastical architecture, and civic buildings, too, the only style. Pugin was certain that architecture both reflected and moulded the spirit of the age, and he decided that church architecture should shape the culture of his own time.

Faced with a phalanx of post-Napoleonic, Classical Greek architectural styles, Pugin declared that Gothic was the only true ENGLISH NATIONAL STYLE. He believed that this was the hallmark of the ancient pre-Reformation Church. In his view, everything had gone wrong at the Reformation, with the introduction of the pagan Classical style that had dominated England's architecture ever since. This was echoed by Pugin's own Roman Catholicism (his father was an emigré who had fled the French Revolution, or at any rate its economic effects), and much of his work was commissioned by the newly emancipated Roman Catholic Church and its patrons.

Having caught the wave of a national mood of *furor gothicus*, Pugin applied his boundless energy to the cause. A draughtsman of incomparable skill, he worked with unbelievable speed and energy.

Whereas Classical church interiors tended towards uniformity, Pugin favoured variety and the 'appropriate' treatment of iron, wood, fabrics, precious metals and painted decoration (this meant that they should adhere to his own precepts of pure medieval design).

He declared principles of SINCERITY, DECORUM and TRUTH, believing that everything in a building must be what it appears to be: staircases should be visible from the outside of a building, indicated by the disposition of windows in a wall or tower, rather than being subservient to a symmetrical scheme or design. In a most characteristic way, he was convinced that the builders themselves must be high-minded and that there was to be no swearing among the bricklayers. Surely a tall order, even on a church building site.

Pugin subscribed to the theory that the Gothic style grows from simple Early English through the Decorated at its zenith and declines into flat-arched Perpendicular. From these three Gothic periods, Pugin chose his own digested form of Early English for remote areas and projects with limited funds because it was economical, simple and primitive. He used Decorated for high-status, big-budget projects. For Pugin, Perpendicular was beyond the pale: it meant decline and decay.

Enthusiasm for Pugin Gothic swept the nation in spite of the fact that it was based on dubious logic and faulty history. Excitement was more important than perfect understanding.

Part of the revival led by Pugin was a Romantic obsession with all things liturgical. The ritual of the early Church was seen as being central to expressing the Mysteries of Faith. A devotion to the sacred trappings of the Eucharist went hand in hand with the change of emphasis from pulpit and sermon back to high altar and Communion. Thus pyx and thurifer, reserved sacrament and baldacchino appeared once again in England's parish churches. The jug, flagon and chalice, which, in the seventeenth century, had become nearly identical to domestic vessels, again took on the GEM-STUDDED FILIGREE GLAMOUR of the pre-Reformation altar. These, together with the vestments worn by priests and acolytes, are vital costumes and props in the drama of the nineteenth-century Gothic Revival church.

In 1840, the single-minded and phenomenally energetic Pugin began to design the 'most complete parish church since the time of Edward I', St Giles Cheadle. This Roman Catholic church is a masterpiece in the Decorated style and was probably the most admired and emulated of all Victorian churches. The interior is coloured all over, with patterned tiles, wall painting, an Easter Sepulchre and those most despised of Popish fripperies: reredos, sedilia with piscina, and screen with coving, parapet and rood. Visible for many a mile is the tall steeple prodding the LOWERING CLOUDS EAST OF STOKE-ON-TRENT.

While Pugin clearly ruled the roost with his early Gothic Revival, he was not the only innovative architect of the early Victorian era. This period also sees the work of a young G.E. Street, Sir Robert Smirke and, in Edinburgh, William Playfair.

There were exceptions to the Gothic rule – St Mary and St Nicholas, Wilton (1844), being one of them. Ill at ease in a polite Wiltshire market town, it is distinct from most other churches you will have seen in England: set well back from the most urban of park railings, it has a cool Italianate façade in austere dove-grey. Closer inspection, however, reveals an OUTSCALED JEWEL-BOX of Romanesque decoration: barley-sugar (known as 'solomonic') columns on recumbent lions, a frieze rising up the gable and down again, a big rose window, and a campanile attached to the church by a long, low gallery where no two columns are the same. Inside, there is a big west gallery and a chancel with a mosaic pavement. Gathered from the Continent are original ancient Roman columns from the temple of Venus at Porto Venere, a pulpit on black marble columns with carved capitals, exotic doors, a font, and stained glass. Although this exercise of wild *Rundbogenstil* is far removed from Pugin's sanctimonious version of Gothic design, it is every bit as whole-hearted, convinced and lavish.

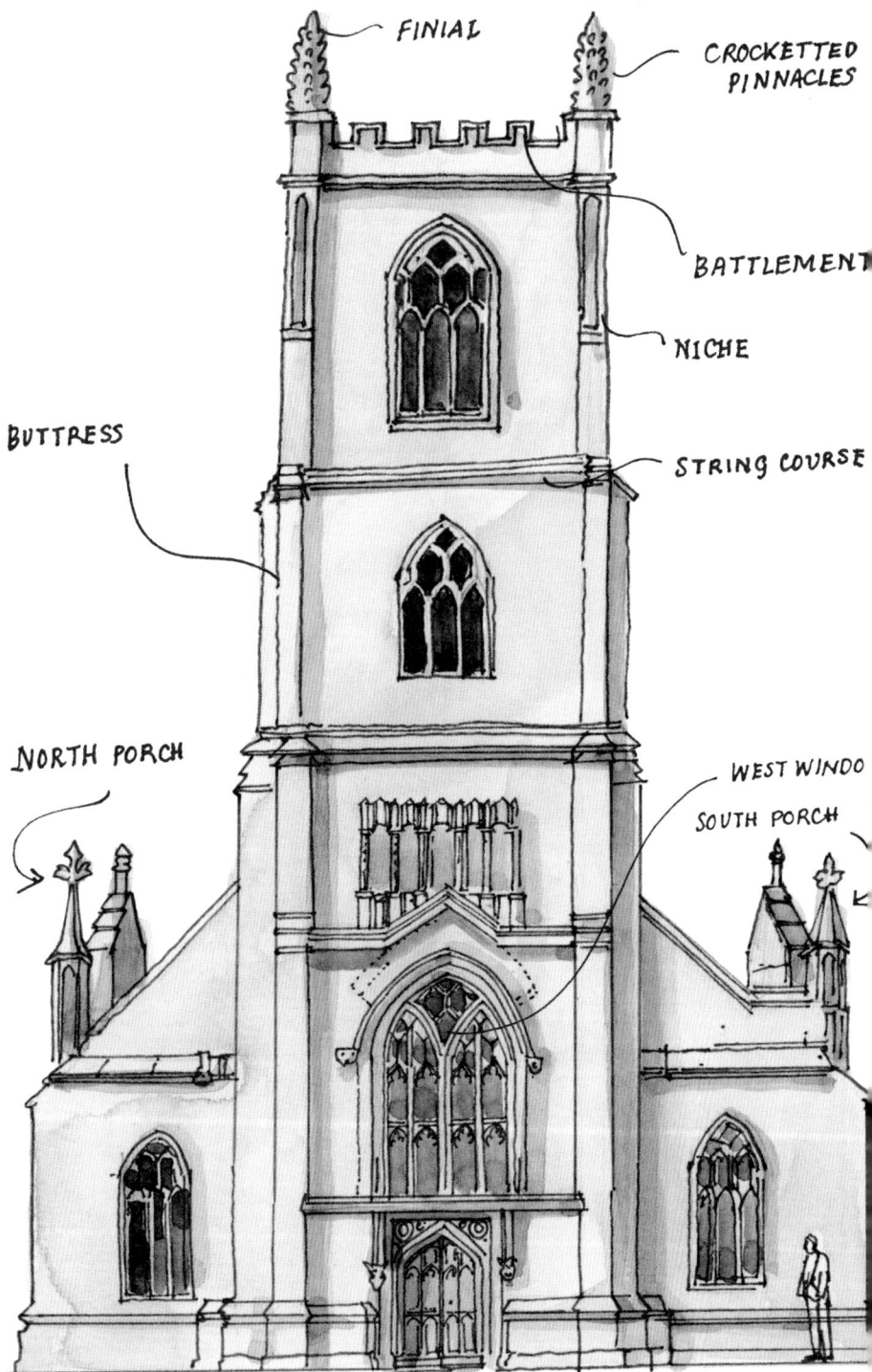

FINIAL

CROCKETTED PINNACLES

BATTLEMENT

NICHE

BUTTRESS

STRING COURSE

NORTH PORCH

WEST WINDO

SOUTH PORCH

K

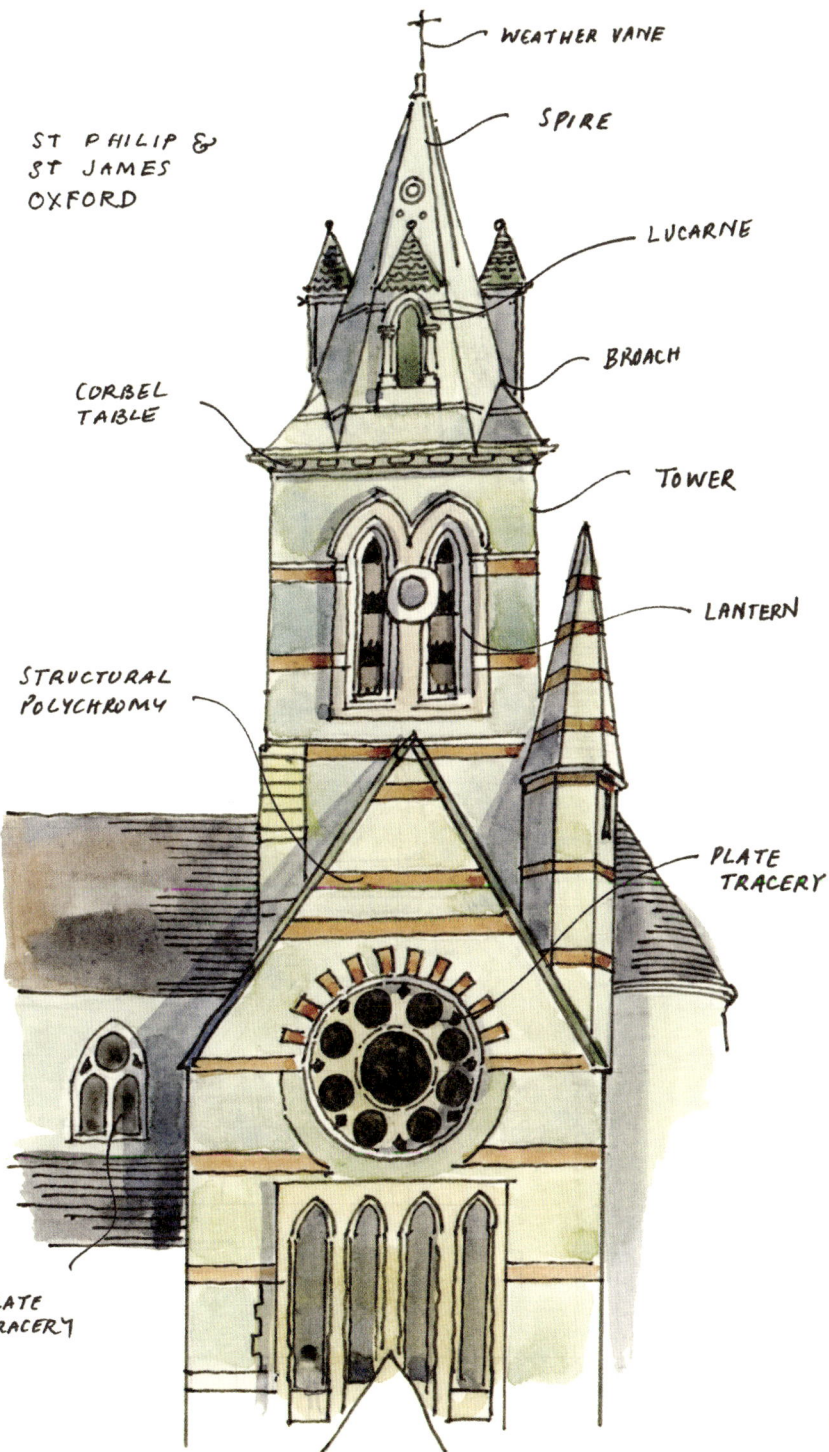

WEATHER VANE

SPIRE

LUCARNE

BROACH

TOWER

LANTERN

PLATE TRACERY

ST PHILIP &
ST JAMES
OXFORD

CORBEL
TABLE

STRUCTURAL
POLYCHROMY

PLATE
TRACERY

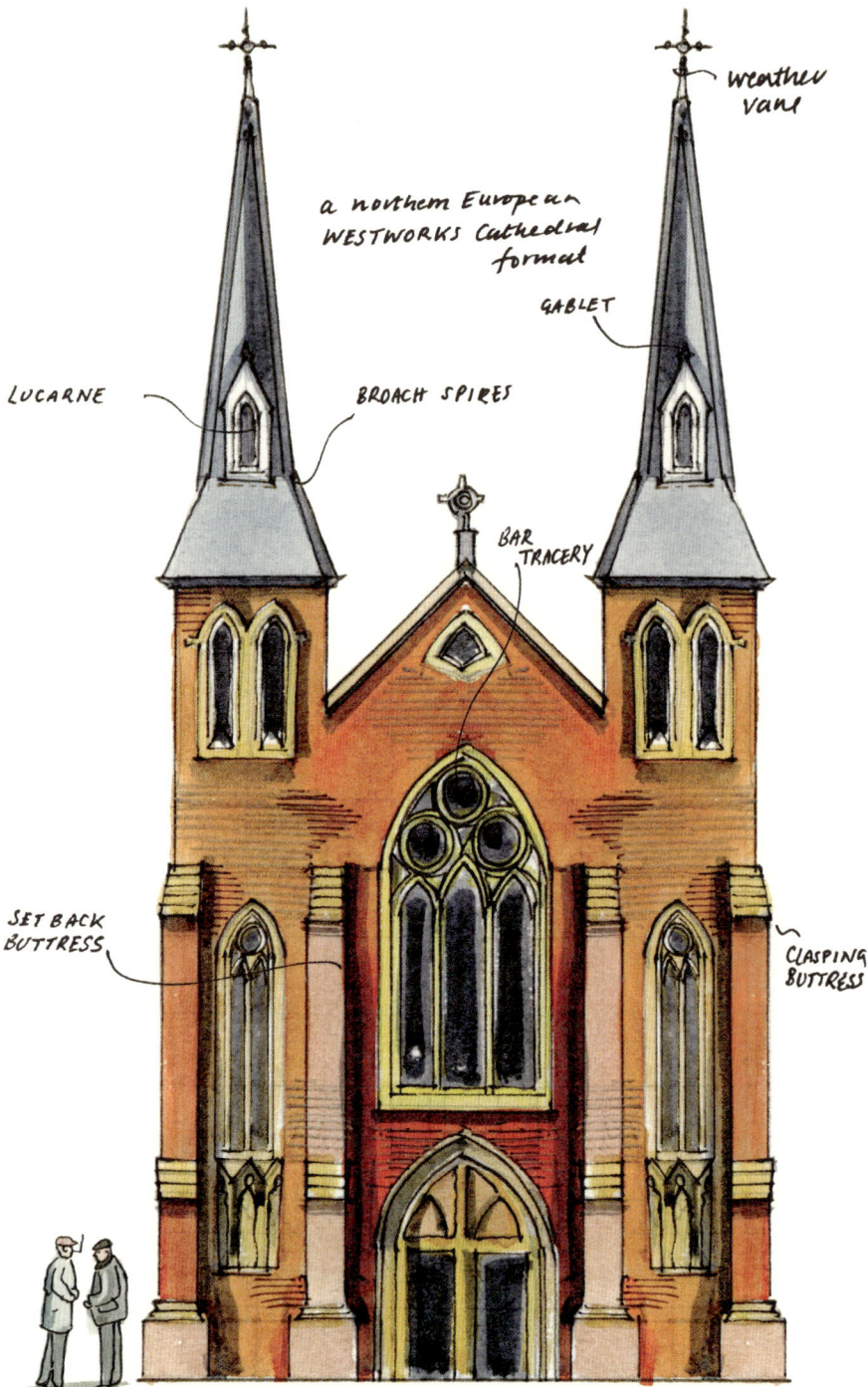

weather vane

a northern European WESTWORKS Cathedral format

GABLET

LUCARNE

BROACH SPIRES

BAR TRACERY

SET BACK BUTTRESS

CLASPING BUTTRESS

ST CHAD'S · BIRMINGHAM · A·W·N·PUGIN · 1841

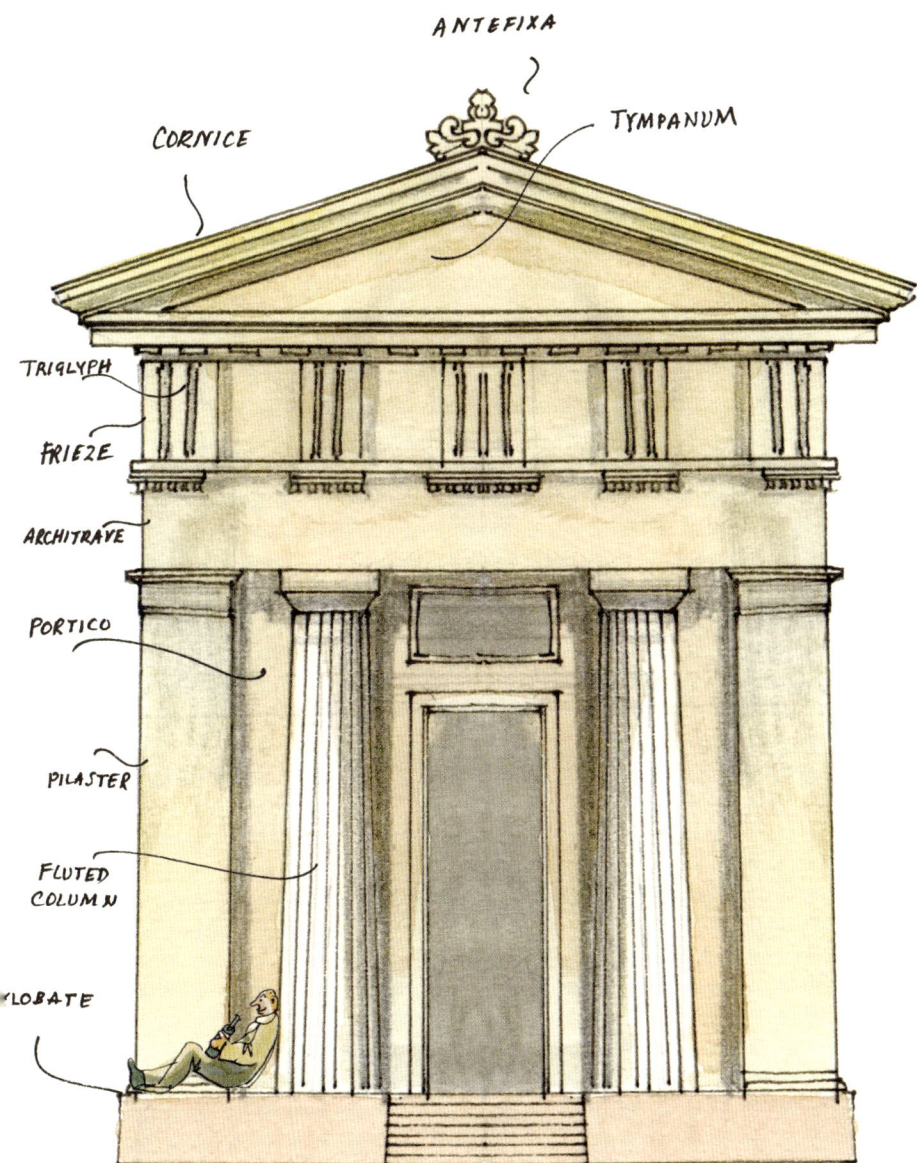

A GRECIAN DORIC TEMPLE
AS R·C·CHURCH· a CLASH of CULTURE

ANTEFIXA

CORNICE

TYMPANUM

TRIGLYPH

FRIEZE

ARCHITRAVE

PORTICO

PILASTER

FLUTED COLUMN

LOBATE

St FRANCIS XAVIER'S · HEREFORD · CHARLES DAY · 1839

These are the
LITURGICAL
FITTINGS of the
REVIVED ANGLICAN
CHURCH... some,
like the candlestick
below, come from
Roman Catholic
Countries in
SOUTHERN EUROPE

GOTHIC
REVIVAL
CHALICE

STATUE of
ST THOMAS
à BECKET with
DRAMATIC
REPRESENTATION
of his
MARTYRDOM

A COUNTER-
-WEIGHTED
FONT COVER

MOTHERS UNION BANNER ... THE
PARISH ENGAGED IN THE CHURCH

M St. MARY U

Mother's Union

DELLA
ROBBIA
PLAQUE
(much
donated
by those
returning
from
Florence
where many
reproductions
of these
were made)

key fitting of
The Revived
Church

STATIONS OF THE CROSS

6

UBIQUITOUS
HYMN NUMBER BOARD

HYMNS

2 1 1

3 7 3

HIGH VICTORIAN

The Great Exhibition of the Industry of All Nations, 1851, was presided over by Queen Victoria's consort, Prince Albert, and showcased by the engineering genius of Paxton's Crystal Palace in Hyde Park. The huge financial success of this enterprise gave rise to the museums of South Kensington; built in memory of Albert, the Blameless Prince (who, despite his austere Germanic virtue, died in 1861), these followed the example of the exhibition space of the Crystal Palace. Most colourful among them is the Natural History Museum (1881). It has an unexpected façade of buff and grey terracotta in a generous Romanesque style, which is inhabited by appropriate sculptures of birds, beasts and plants. This, together with the gilded Albert Memorial in Kensington Gardens (1872), is characteristic of the HIGH VICTORIAN STYLE.

At this mid-century moment, John Ruskin published his *Seven Lamps of Architecture* (1849). This hugely influential work, which immortalises Augustus Pugin's architectural principles, begins by trumpeting that the history of architecture is the history of the world. Ruskin pleads for a universal national style, a concept that had been on the mind of British politicians while the 1840 Houses of Parliament were being commissioned. It continued to be a live issue at the Foreign Office, which was at the centre of the proliferating Empire. The governing caste were searching for appropriate architectural clothing for their rule, regarding the Classical style as both too foreign and too secular. Ruskin promoted the Decorated style, as represented by the cathedrals of Lincoln and Wells – he described Lincoln as 'out and out our most precious piece of architecture'.

The *Seven Lamps* called for STRUCTURAL POLYCHROMY. This mellifluous phrase is key to the architecture of the late nineteenth century, as well as being a good one to trip off the tongue. It describes the use of many and varied materials of different shades, and walls coursed like geological layers: yellow brick, above sandstone, above grey brick, above red brick, and so on. Ruskin preferred coloured materials to applied colour; he loved ornament, and different qualities of surface and light. He yearned for the coloured marble of Italy, but found Palladio's Venetian churches 'disgusting' (they were, for him, the epitome of all things un-Gothic, unromantic and, as churches, irreligious).

It was in this environment that William Butterfield (architect of Keble College, Oxford) designed the Ecclesiologically sponsored All Saints on Margaret Street, London (1851). The church was sited among houses and shops much less respectable than the ones that are there now, and against this dingy background the church was an experiment of red brick and stone bands, voussoirs and diaperwork. This was ground-breaking design, lively and dynamic after so much monochrome stone.

Perhaps All Saints says it all. On approaching the church, you are mindful only of the high, slender, sheer steeple with its broached spire, but, once inside, you are dazzled. Because of the cramped site, there is no east window nor windows in the north aisle, but there is plenty of room for decoration instead: wall tiles of green, red, black and cream, encaustic floor tiles, a delicate ironwork screen, inlaid marble, a polychromatic pulpit and coloured glass. They were recognisable elements, but the design as a whole was startlingly new for its time. The Tractarian chancel is high, wide, deep and raised, the nave piers have red shafts on black bases. The church is no mere imitation of past styles and motifs; it is an original, ingenious and imaginative work speaking in the architectural language of medieval Europe. It became an influential archetype.

Also by Butterfield is brick-built Keble College Chapel (1863), striped to the heavens, the gift of the GUANO-TRADE-ENRICHED Gibbs family, who encouraged the renewal of Christian zeal in Oxford. Then came the chapel at Rugby School, Warwickshire (1870), and also All Saints in Babbacombe, Devon (1874). These were in a similar vein and, more importantly, begot hundreds of similar churches, which housed congregations from Stoke-on-Trent to Hackney Wick.

From a poor area by the canal in Paddington rose the strange, tall, striped belfry and stone spire of G.E. Street's St Mary Magdalene (begun 1867) near the station. The slums have been cleared and the church now stands isolated, but it must have been an astonishing declaration of war on poverty, illiteracy and ignorance. Indeed, the powerful contrast between the gilded and painted interiors of the Oxford Movement-inspired churches – such as St Barnabas, Jericho, Oxford (1869), whose Italianate tower rises above the artisan housing of north Oxford like the CATHEDRAL OF TORCELLO IN THE VENETIAN LAGOON – and the low terraces that housed their parishioners still seems remarkable. The 'glimpse of Heaven' afforded to the growing urban working class, who never saw the blue skies under which their grandfathers had followed the plough, was a powerful weapon against the basically anti-establishment influence of ultra-Protestant Nonconformism.

New Nonconformist churches had appeared in parallel with the expanding urban working class, whose attitudes and emerging political radicalism Nonconformism could accommodate. Churches like the Bethesda Chapel in Stoke-on-Trent (1819) had pews to seat two thousand. The Methodists, Unitarians and other denominations played fast and loose with architectural styles, revelling in eclecticism with a whole-hearted lack of restraint: it was in the Nonconformist cathedrals of the industrial North and Midlands that Classicism first saw a renaissance.

However, the renewal of worship and churchmanship in the mid-nineteenth century was not all masonry, glass and brass. Church vestments were subject to a similar revival. The basic set of vestments included the CHASUBLE (a development of the ancient Roman *vestore*, or woollen poncho), the STOLE (a band of coloured cloth about nine feet in length) and the AMICE (a strip of fine linen, worn as 'helmet of salvation to extinguish the fiery dance of the DIABOLICAL INCURSIONS OF THE DEVIL'). In the eyes of the resolutely Protestant, these were seen as seriously 'Roman' and were put aside in favour of a watered-down version of sixteenth-century Puritan clerical dress.

Almost every style took a turn on the busy mahogany drawing desks of nineteenth-century church architects, from the Romanesque Italianate of Ravenna to pyramidical fantasie from Egypt, or from neo-Norman to Byzantine. In Glasgow, the Caledonia Road Church of 1857 is determinedly Classical, built on a massive podium, and is the work of the rightly called 'Greek' Thomson; it stands high above the street like an Acropolis – but with an Egyptian tower – and inside it is brightly decorated and exotically ornamented.

In 1880, Norman Shaw's St Michael and All Angels in Bedford Park, London, introduced a Domestic Revival. The outside of the church, with balustrades and lantern, is hardly distinguishable from a village hall and, indeed, the interior woodwork is painted green and feels secular, familiar and cosy. It sets an eclectic note for the rest of Bedford Park, a signal move away from the nearby serried ranks of brick-built terraces which so dominated the fabric of fast-growing metropolitan London.

England's relationship with the Industrial Revolution that had so shaped it was never totally peaceful. This found its most extreme expression in William Morris and the Arts and Crafts Movement, which had spread in tandem with the very industrial powertowns, cottonopolises or satanic mills to which it was a reaction. Miles away from the belching chimneys, St Sophia's in Lower Kingswood, Surrey (1891) is a wonderfully pretty little church by the architect Sidney Barnsley, the east end entirely furnished in mosaic and marble and with nine capitals actually from Byzantium and Ephesus; the decoration on the timber wagon roof and woodwork is by the architect, and executed in ebony and holly with mother of-pearl inlay.

The nineteenth century saw much church restoration, but it was a far cry from the forensic and carefully researched projects undertaken today. This was a period of extreme, perhaps excessive, confidence. The High Victorian period was dominated by zealous Christian architects who saw 'restoration' not just as the work done in stone, wood and plaster, but as a means for promulgating prayer and the celebration of the Eucharist in buildings long neglected. These were buildings to be used, buildings with a purpose, and they were never perceived as museums, even if their restoration was tackled with a historian's obsessive attention to detail. The establishment in 1877 of the Society for the Protection of Ancient Buildings, the leading light of which was William Morris, marked the beginnings of a concern about the unintended destruction wrought by the restorers. These worthy campaigners had wiped away the accretions of the centuries as they exposed masonry always meant to be rendered. This left countless churches in an embarrassed nakedness, a process Morris called 'scraping'. Happily, the scraping and rebuilding century is past, and a builder's board is now usually a good sign when you visit a church.

Amid the enormous building programmes, good Victorian architecture shines out. This great benevolent society dwelt confident and secure in prosperity and peace; it saw and experienced scientific advancement and social reform, improvement in food, clothes and opportunities for travel, and granted the social benefits of churches. Not since medieval times had so many churches been needed and unstintingly provided, endowed and filled.

CAP

ST BARNABAS
JERICHO
OXFORD

NAVE

CLERESTORY

PORCH

ARCADED CLOISTE

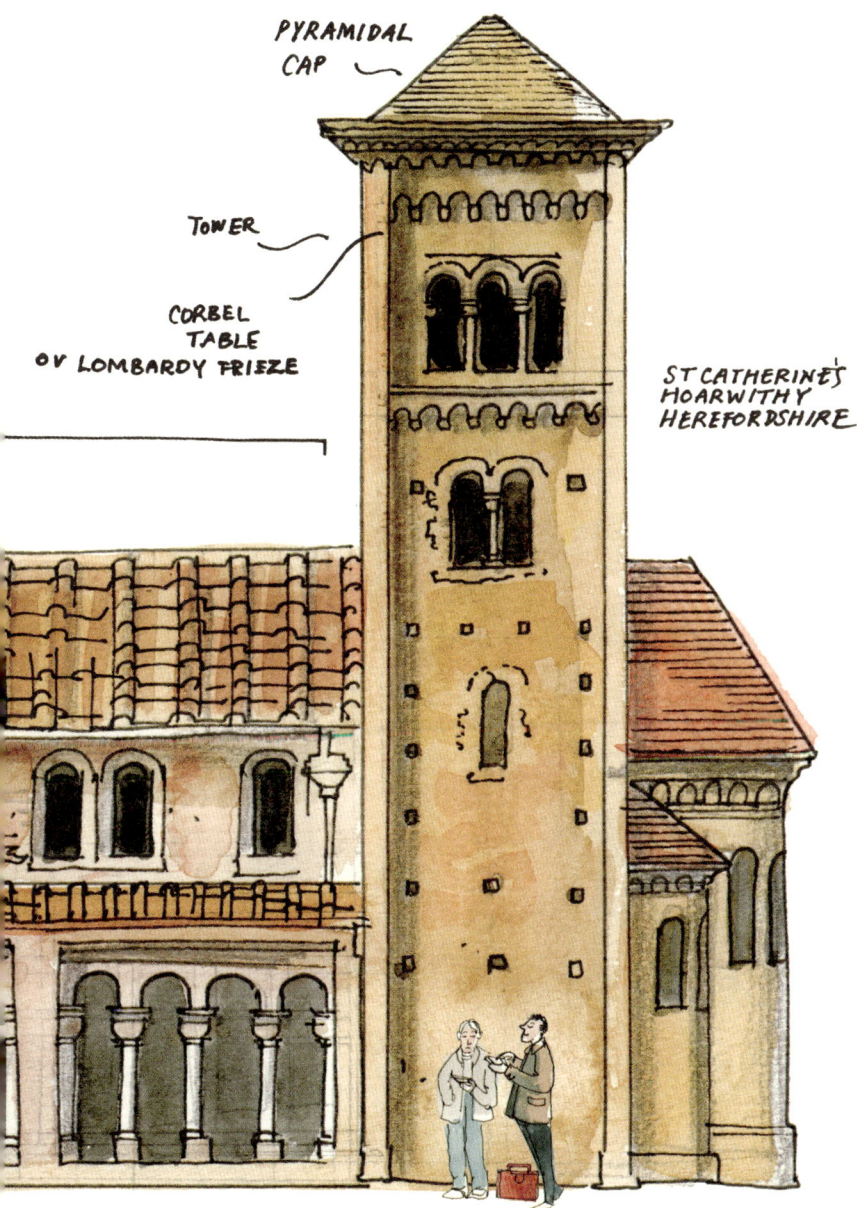

PYRAMIDAL
CAP

TOWER

CORBEL
TABLE
OV LOMBARDY FRIEZE

ST CATHERINES
HOARWITHY
HEREFORDSHIRE

UNITED REFORMED CHURCH
CLAPTON PARK
LONDON

nineteenth-century eclecticism ie
a TOTAL MIX-UP of STYLES. here: CLASSICAL
ITALIANATE, FLEMISH and ROMANESQUE

DORMER

ROMANESQUE
ROUND—
—TOPPED
ARCH

STILTED ARCH

UNITED REFORMED CHURCH · CLAPTON PARK
(a most peculiar porch)

ST CHAD'S HACKNEY POLYCHROMY late tracery

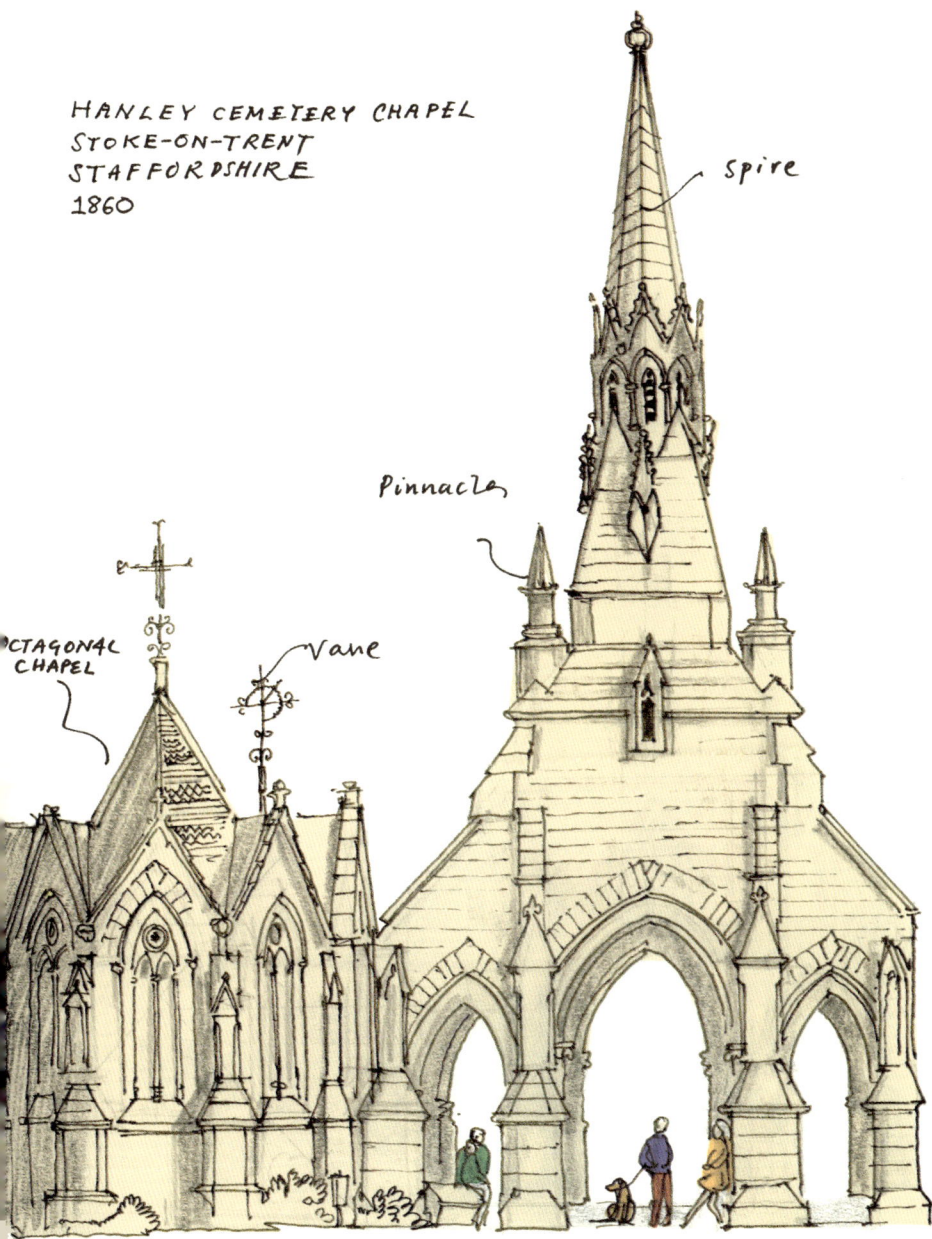

HANLEY CEMETERY CHAPEL
STOKE-ON-TRENT
STAFFORDSHIRE
1860

spire

Pinnacle

Vane

OCTAGONAL
CHAPEL

HIGH ST METHODIST CHURCH
HANLEY. STAFFORDSHIRE
1860

non-conformist Italianate
decorative, polychrome and
inventive

rusticated Pilasters

ERECTED 1860

CAMPANILE

ST JOSEPH'S (R.C.)
BURSLEM
STOKE-ON-TRENT
J.S. BROCKLESBY
1925/27

RAVENNA in
Engineering brick
and cement.

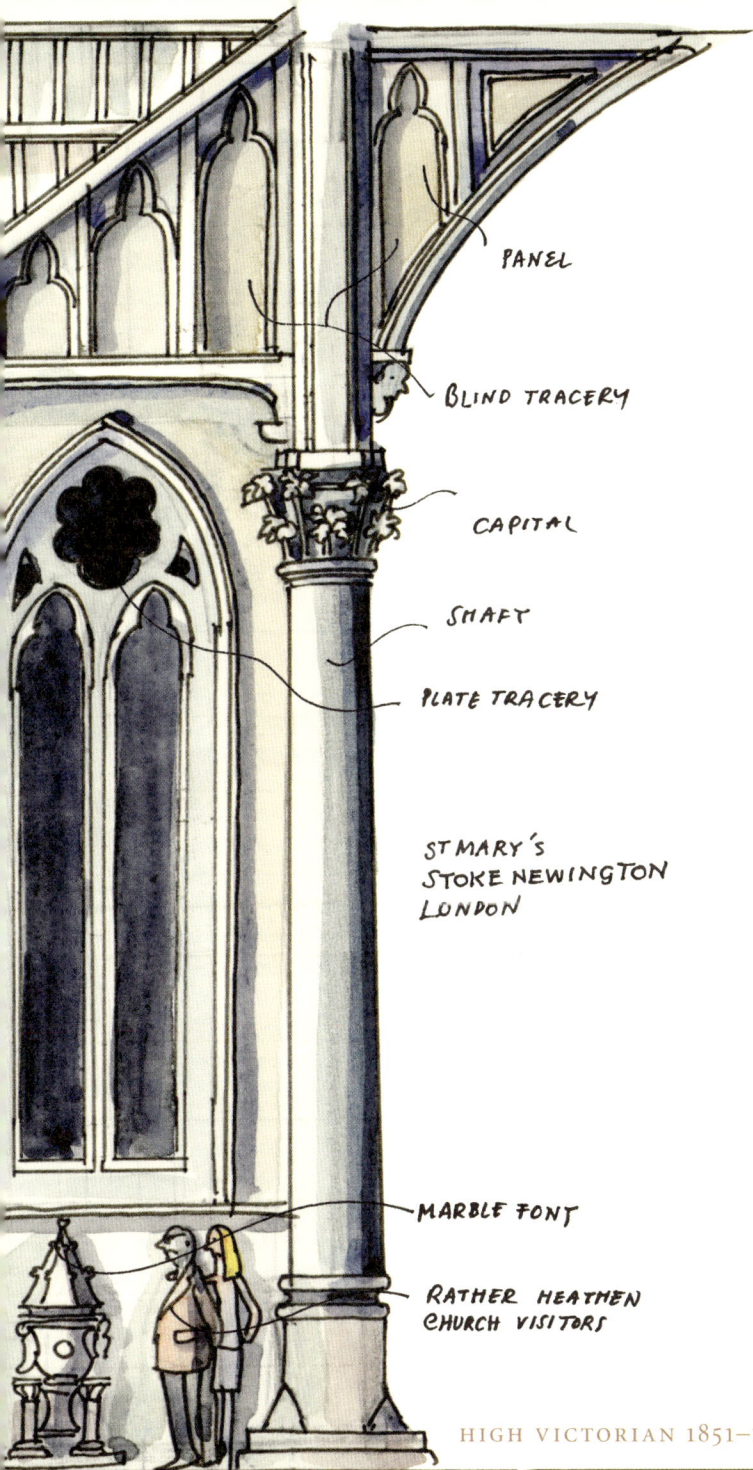

PANEL

BLIND TRACERY

CAPITAL

SHAFT

PLATE TRACERY

ST MARY'S
STOKE NEWINGTON
LONDON

MARBLE FONT

RATHER HEATHEN
CHURCH VISITORS

MODERN

The extraordinary survival of the medieval steeple at the Cathedral of St Michael, Coventry, destroyed by enemy action on 14 November 1940, was particularly inspirational for the architect of the renovation, Basil Spence. Towers and spires are familiar in Victorian churches that hark back to the Middle Ages, but the twentieth century is not famous for such features. Spence incorporated this familiar steeple into his design for the 1962 building, which became the most widely known cathedral of our time.

Spence produced three more churches in the suburbs of Coventry. The bishop wanted good modern buildings built economically, and they are all of concrete, aisle-less and with BARE WALLS. Spence may have abandoned Gothic forms, but his cathedral follows the liturgical tradition of having a long nave and focus on the east end. So, too, does Liverpool's fine Gothic-style Anglican cathedral of 1924 (it was not completed until 1978, thus winning the prize of the last Gothic cathedral in Britain hands down). It is an extraordinary *coup de théâtre*, and a complete vision, something unheard of in Gothic cathedrals built over centuries. Facing it along Hope Street, the Roman Catholic cathedral does something quite different. The church authorities there insisted on an intimate association between congregation and priest, so the high altar had to be visible to everyone. Consequently, the building is centrally planned. It is a 200-foot circle supported by reinforced boomerang-like concrete trusses, and held together by concrete circles. Reaching upwards in a funnel-shape, it is topped by a lantern surrounded by spikes, the glass of which is made by Patrick Reyntiens to an abstract design by John Piper. These are two features that the cathedral shares with most post-war parish churches: a central plan and abstract art.

These INCLUSIVE, enthusiastic and burningly honest reverend places have not yet had time to endear themselves to the public or, at any rate, the church-visiting among them. The post-war Liturgical Movement calls for an auditoria-style church that decisively rejects the entire legacy of church architecture. This will often be made of prefabricated parts bearing either a pyramidal or a low-spreading polygonal roof. The interior resembles an open-plan office, simple and austere. The chairs are often stackable, so as to leave uncluttered space, and there is no physical separation between nave and sanctuary.

However, plenty of fine church buildings have been built since the Second World War. St Andrew's Roman Catholic Church in Craigshill, West Lothian (1968), boasts concentric walls of thin concrete curving up to a sharp point, a kind of abstract tower and steeple. The square William Temple Memorial Church at Wythenshawe, Manchester (1965), has a diagonal internal axis pushing the altar to a corner; its girders and beams are rolled steel, another favoured modern building material, with concrete and brick, all very visible. In 1937, architect Nugent Francis Cachemaille-Day proposed a sensational star-shaped plan for St Michael's Northenden, Lancashire, but the absolutely centrally placed altar, *à la* Liturgical Movement, was refused by the bishop. Such is the changing and confused taste of twentieth-century church design.

Inside churches, there is ceramic, mosaic and tapestry with designs sometimes abstract, sometimes representational. Most powerfully, the Lady Chapel of Coventry Cathedral is dominated by Graham Sutherland's huge Christ, with hands raised. Plate glass is now available in huge sizes, which can transform the possibilities for new window shapes, yet, often, windows are squeezed into UNEXPECTED PLACES and are set at ODD ANGLES. Glass can be engraved or it can be coloured. The production and development of traditional stained glass continues skilfully. It is usually of an abstract, gem-like brightness, with the effect of swirling motion. Dom Charles Norris's colourful 'slabs-of-glass', or *dalle de verre*, which are set in concrete, can form whole walls.

Very much of its time is St Matthew's, Jersey (1934). The church is fitted with glass altar and altar rail, chalice-shaped font, cross, pillars, and screens with images of angels and lilies, all of Art Deco glasswork designed and made by Lalique. Altogether more formal are the elemental geometric shapes, planes and volumes of St Paul's, Harringay (1993), constrained to rise no higher than nearby terraced houses. The church is of red brick, steel and reconstituted stone, the interior white with black furniture, with both rough and smooth surfaces.

Beside these 'progressive' churches, we can set Stephen Dykes Bower's church of St John's in Newbury, Berkshire (1957). It is based on a conservative plan of mild red and grey brick, nave satisfactorily separated from sanctuary, with a baldacchino and an ambulatory round the altar. Another reaction to Modern design is the restrained Classicism of James Fletcher Watson's All Saints in Bawdeswell, Norfolk, of 1953: it is a perfect stripped-down neo-Georgian church.

But these are break-outs from the orthodoxy of increasingly industrial specifications. As we have become LESS CONVINCED that Modernism is the answer to all architectural questions, so our confidence in alternatives has faded. With a diluted Gothic arch as its unhappy symbol, the Church has resorted to the lowest common denominator in this, the least productive and least pleasing era of church-building.

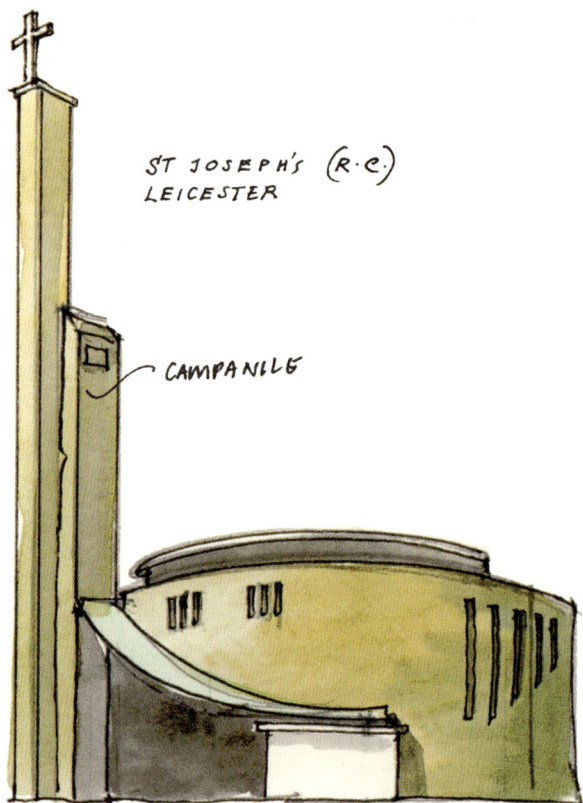

ST JOSEPH'S (R·C·)
LEICESTER

CAMPANILE

BELL TOWER

PORCH

ST JOHN The BAPTIST · MAESBURY · OSWESTRY · SHROPSHIRE   Y-TRACERY

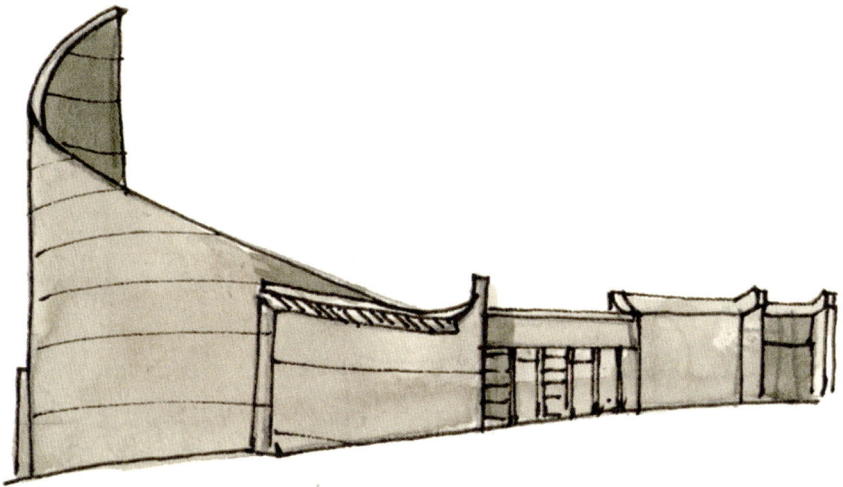

ST ANDREW'S · LIVINGSTON

COVENTRY CATHEDRAL

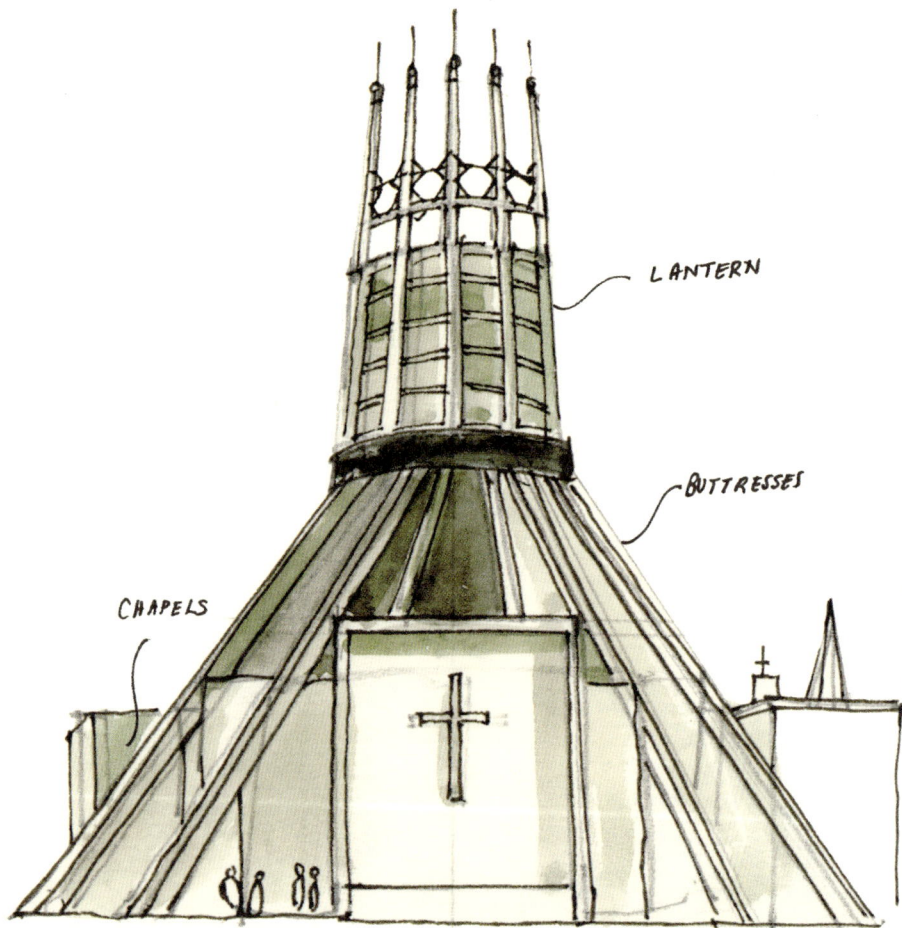

R·C· CATHEDRAL
LIVERPOOL

LANTERN

BUTTRESSES

CHAPELS

METHODIST CHURCH · SALTNEY
CHESHIRE

LORETTO CHAPEL
EAST LOTHIAN

NTON UNITARIAN · CARDIFF

EXEMPLARS

IN WHICH

CHURCHES

ARE ARRANGED IN ORDER of CHRONOLOGY

ST JOHN THE EVANGELIST
ESCOMB · Cº DURHAM · 680

ST PETER with ST CUTHB.
MONKWEARMOUTH
Cº DURHAM
LOWER TOWER · 675
UPPER TOWER · 1000

ALL SAINTS · BRIXWORTH
NORTHAMPTONSHIRE · 680
(a stonker, just off the A508)

HEATH CHAPEL · SHROPSHIRE

⑫

ST MARGARET · HALES · NORFOLK
1150

ST MARY & ST DAVID
KILPECK · SHROPSHIRE · 1135–1150

DORNOCH
CATHEDRAL
SCOTLAND
⑬ & 1835

ST HILDA'S
HARTLEPOOL ⑬

S.DOOR ⑫
W.FRONT ⑬
& 1867

LLANDAFF
CATHEDRAL
WALES

TEWKESBURY
ABBEY
GLOUCESTERSHIRE
NAVE ⑫
VAULT ⑭

ABBEY DORE
HEREFORDSHIRE
1175-1220

ALL SAINTS
WOODCHURCH
KENT
EARLY 13

TYDD
St GILES
CAMBRIDGESHIRE
EARLY 13

St ANTHONY
IN ROSELAND
CORNWALL
12, 13
& 1850

ST MARY'S
HARTLEY
WESTPALL
HAMPSHIRE

C14 TIMBERS

ST MARY & ALL SAINTS
CAR COLSTON
NOTTINGHAMSHIRE

EAST WINDOW 1330

ST NICHOLAS'S · NEW ROMNEY
KENT · EARLY C14

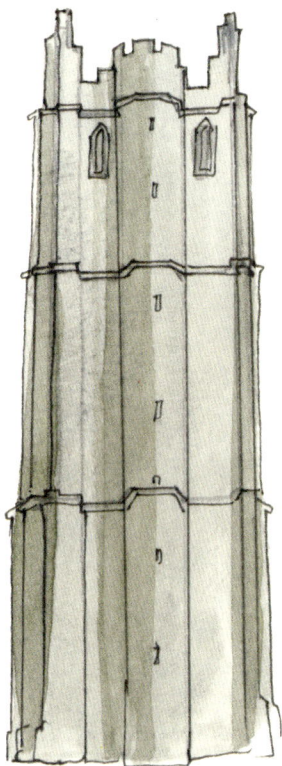

ST ANDREW'S
IPPLEPEN
DEVONSHIRE · 1450

GLOUCESTER CATHEDRAL
1350 — 1360

BRIDGE CHAPEL · WAKEFIELD
YORKSHIRE · 1357

MARTHAM · E · NORFOLK
C14 & C15

ERPINGHAM GATE
NORWICH CATHEDRAL
1416 ~ 1425

ST JOHN'S · YEOVIL · SOMERSET
1380 ~ 1400

KING'S COLLEGE · CAMBRIDGE · c.1500

ST PETER & ST PAUL
SHEVIOCK
CORNWALL
C13, C14
& 1850

ST MARGARET'S · STOKE GOLDING · LEICESTERSHIRE
1280–1290

ST HELEN'S · SEFTON · MERSEYSIDE · 1500–1540

PEMBROKE
COLLEGE
CHAPEL
CAMBRIDGE
1663

HOLY-TRINITY
STAUNTON
HAROLD
LEICESTERSHIRE
1653—1665

ST MARY MAGDALENE
MILTON KEYNES
1678

ST AIDAN'S
BILLINGE
MANCHESTER
1718

CANONGATE KIRK
EDINBURGH · 1691

ST BENET'S · PAUL'S WHARF · LONDON
1677–1683

ST MARY'S · DAIRSIE · FIFE
1621

ST ANDREW'S · GUNTON
NORFOLK · (R. ADAM) · 1780

KIRKANDREW
CUMBRIA
1775

ST MARY'S · WARWICK · 1698—1704

PORTMAHOMACK TARBAT (RC) · 1756
BELCOTE 1700

ST MARY'S
WEST COWES
ISLE OF WIGHT · 1816

THE OCTAGON · NORWICH · 1756

KILLEAN · TAYINLOAN · ARGYLLSHIRE · 1787

ST PETER &
ST LEONARD
HORBURY
WEST
YORKSHIRE
(JOHN CARR)
1791

ST MARY'S · WALSALL
(R.C.) 1825-1827

HOLY TRINITY
MARYLEBONE Rd
(JOHN SOANE) · 1828

ST PETER
BRIGHT?
(C · BARRY) · 18.

HOLY TRINITY · THEALE · BERKSHIRE · 1820-1822
TOWER 1827-1832

ST MARY'S WILTON · WILTSHIRE
(THOS WYATT) · 1845

ST GEORGE'S · DONCASTER
(George GILBERT SCOTT)
1858

ST PETER'S · DAYLESFORD
GLOUCESTERSHIRE · 1860

ST MICHAEL & ALL ANGELS
BOOTON · NORFOLK
(Rev WHITWELL ELWIN) 1875 – 1891

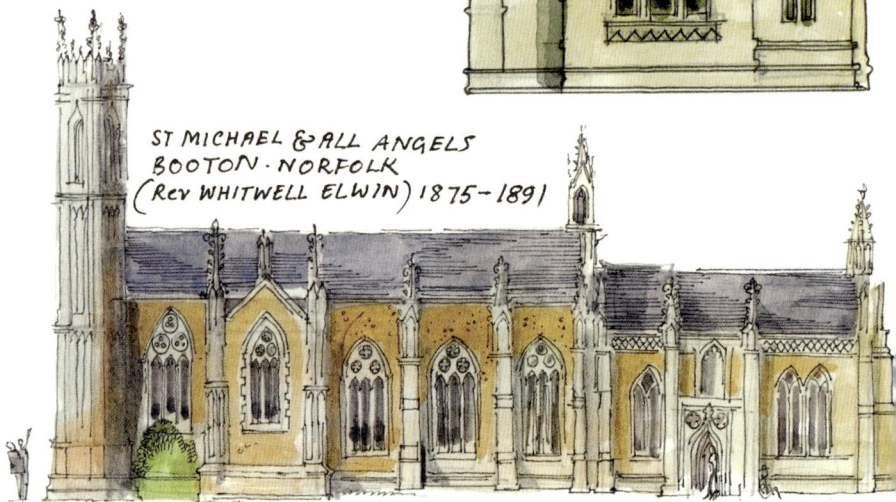

METHODIST CHURCH
OVERSTRAND
NORFOLK
(EDWIN LUTYENS)
1898

WESTMINSTER CATHEDRAL
JOHN FRANCIS BENTLEY

1903

ST MICHAEL & ALL ANGELS
NORTHENDEN · MANCHESTER
1937

ST NICHOLAS'S · BURNAGE
MANCHESTER · 1932

SCOTLAND

THE NORTH

N.B
THESE MAPS USE the
OLD COUNTY BOUNDARIES,
PERHAPS NOT VERY
GOOGLE-MAP-FRIENDLY
BUT VILLAGES ARE ALL EASY
TO FIND!

THE MIDLANDS

WALES &
the MARCHES

EAST
ANGLIA

LONDON &
the SOUTH

THE WEST

The countryside was formed by volcanoes, Romans and enlightened landowners, and we see it all through the eyes of Sir Walter Scott's Romances. The Borders now shelter picturesque ruined rose-coloured monasteries. Eighteenth-century landowners converted theatrically sited tower-houses into elegant country houses and transformed the mud or dry-stone rubble walls and thatch into the neat single-storey symmetrical houses that now line every village. Beyond the Roman Antonine Wall (AD80), travelling from east to west, we discover eighteenth-century enclosures and the Georgian towns and cities of the Golden Age of Scottish culture, which are in stark contrast with the wild, rough, lonely Highlands and Islands that fade into the Atlantic sunset.

1) St Magnus Cathedral, Kirkwall, Orkney
2) Dornoch Cathedral
3) Tarbat Old Church, Portmahomack
4) Iona Abbey, Argyll
5) 'Round Church', Kilarrow, Islay
6) St Vincent Street Church, Glasgow
7) Queen's Park Parish Church, Glasgow
8) Dunblane Cathedral
9) St Ninian's Cathedral, Perth
10) Dunfermline Abbey
11) Dalgety Bay Chapel
12) St Mary's, Dairsie
13) St Regulus, St Andrews
14) St Michael's, Linlithgow
15) St Andrew's, Livingston
16) Canongate Kirk, Edinburgh
17) Loretto School Chapel, Musselburgh
18) Rosslyn Chapel
19) Jedburgh Abbey
20) Crichton Memorial Church

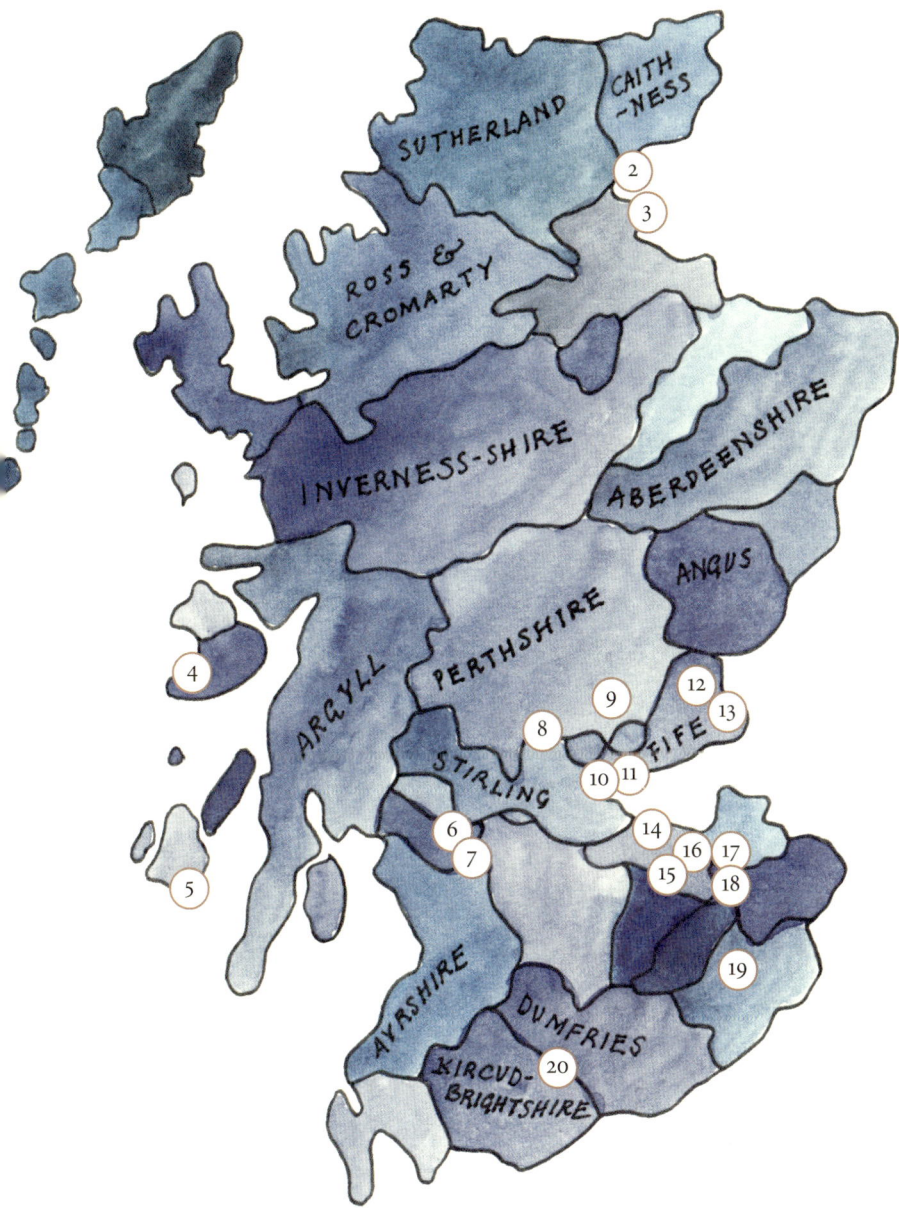

CAITH-NESS

SUTHERLAND

ROSS & CROMARTY

INVERNESS-SHIRE

ABERDEENSHIRE

ANGUS

PERTHSHIRE

ARGYLL

FIFE

STIRLING

AYRSHIRE

DUMFRIES

KIRCVD-BRIGHTSHIRE

The NORTH

In the north-west, red limestone churches dating back to the earliest Christian settlements contained by slate and stone walls merge into the grey and smoke-blackened chapels of the industrial north-east coast. Before the Norman conquest, this was the most sophisticated part of the country, and sculptured Saxon crosses bear witness to this, but after uprisings the Normans harried it and left their mark in the churches with boldly carved stone fonts. In the nineteenth century, architects were called in to minister to new huge cities. The North is, away from the grand town churches, quiet and sparsely furnished with gaunt churches, with the exception of Holderness with its large, elegant, medieval parishes.

1

CUMB*

1) Kirkandrews
2) St Mary's, Wreay
3) Hexham Abbey
4) St Peter's, Monkwearmouth
5) Escomb Saxon Church
6) St Hilda's, Hartlepool
7) St Mary and All Saints, Whalley
8) St Helen's, Sefton
9) Roman Catholic Cathedral, Liverpool
10) St Aidan's, Billinge
11) St Francis, Wythenshawe
12) St Nicholas's, Burnage, Manchester
13) Ripon Cathedral
14) St Peter and St Leonard, Horbury
15) St Mary's, Birkin
16) Chantry Chapel of St Mary, Wakefield Bridge
17) St George's Minster, Doncaster
18) St Patrick's, Patrington

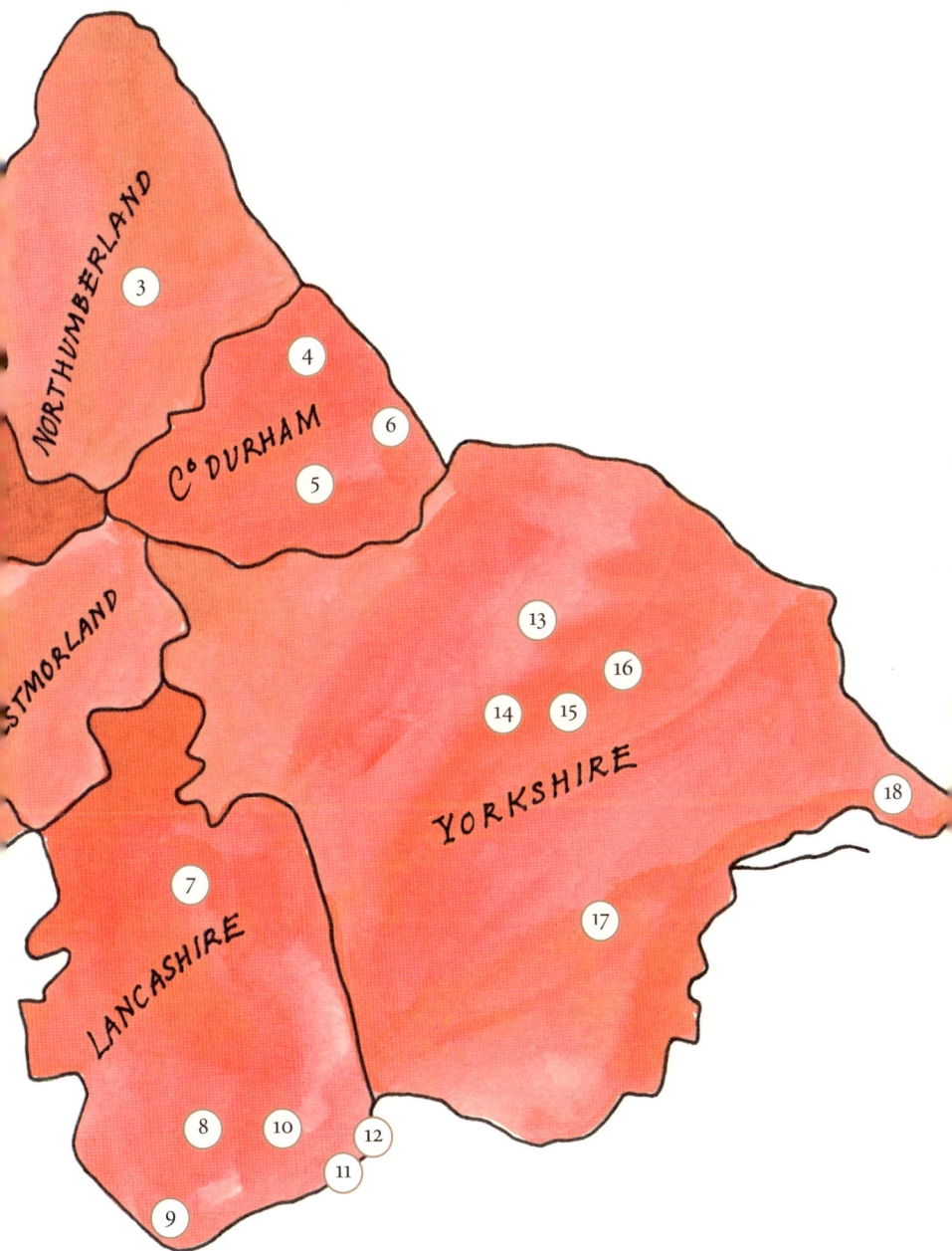

WALES & The MARCHES

The Celts, among the first Christians in the land, were chased by Romans into this rough country, and their later movements were monitored by medieval castles and fortress churches. The Industrial Revolution began in the woods and rivers here and, thenceforth, slate quarries and coalmines characterised the landscape. Today, however, this is the sleepiest part of the country, farms are secluded, red-earthed fields smaller. Churches are pink sandstone and timber-framed, and Methodist chapels abound. The land is soft and rolling in the east, mountainous as it reaches the sea in the north and, following the M4, busy and industrious over the Severn Bridge.

1) Capel Newydd, Nanhoron
2) St Mary's, Llanegryn
3) Llanaber Chapel
4) St Eilian's, Llaneilian
5) St Mary's, Mold
6) All Saints, Gresford
7) Rhug Chapel
8) St John's, Maesbury
9) St Mary's, Shrewsbury
10) St David's Cathedral
11) St Mary's, Carew
12) St Mary's, Kidwelly
13) St Illtud's, Llantwit Major
14) Llandaff Cathedral, Cardiff
15) St Mary's, Nash
16) St Aeddan's, Bettws Newydd
17) St Peter's, Peterchurch

18) St Francis Xavier's, Hereford
19) Abbey Dore
20) St Mary and St David, Kilpeck
21) St Catherine's, Hoarwithy

10

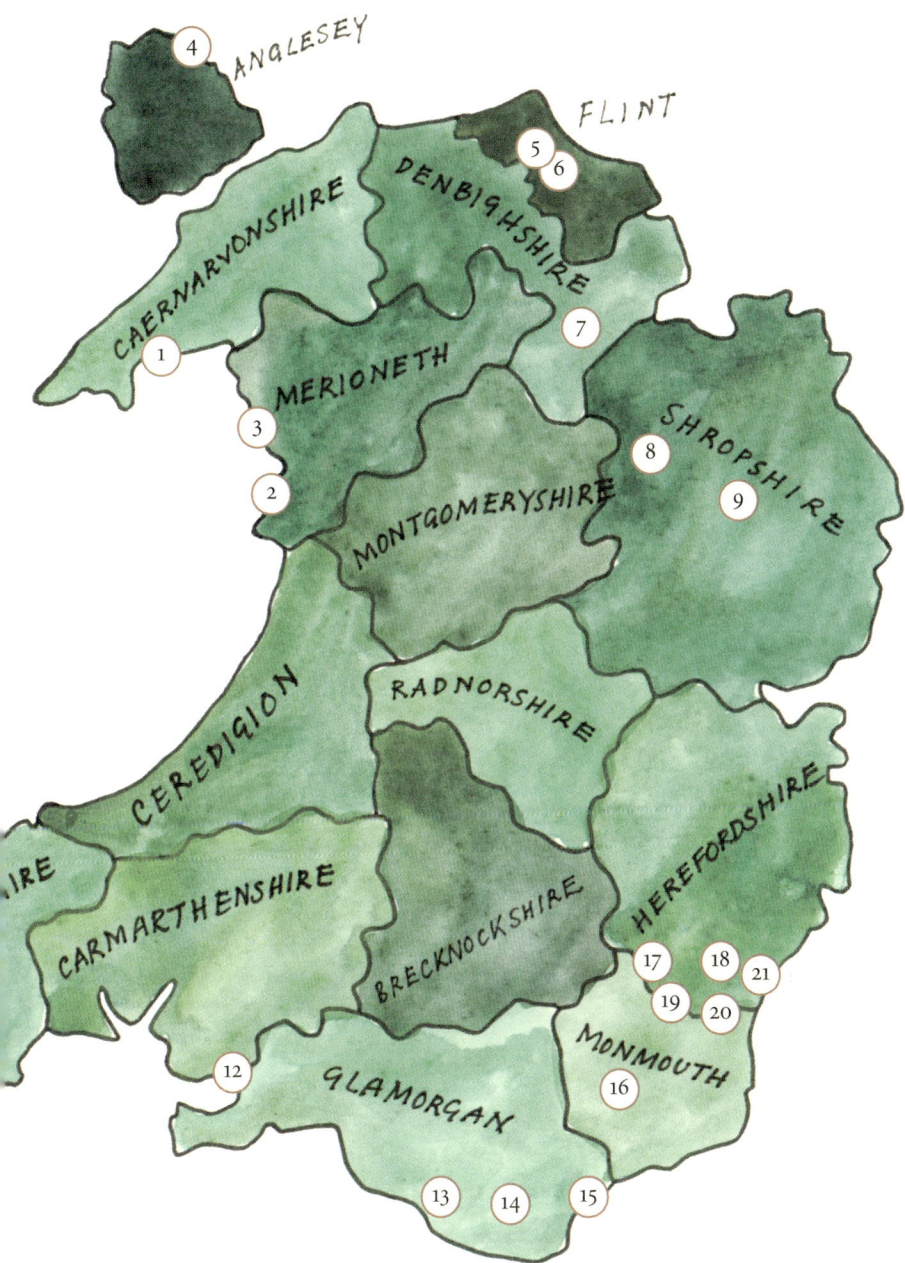

The MIDLANDS

The centre of this Midland ironwork region is busy industry, crossed by Roman roads and commercial eighteenth-century canals. The churches are pale silvery limestone with deep-brown ironstone towers and Colleyweston slates. Their steeples became models for the Victorian churches of London. In the chalky south, where the Thames grows in size, there is the academic romance of Oxford and, further north, there is darker mystery in the Peak District and ballads of the bow-and-arrow kind in Sherwood Forest. In the north of the region were the famous medieval alabaster workshops, which spread their wares countrywide. Parishes here have always been large, and the agriculture is the richest and creamiest in the land.

1) High Street Methodist Church, Hanley
2) St Mary's, Ingestre
3) St Chad's, Birmingham
4) Coventry Cathedral
5) St Mary's, Warwick
6) All Saints, Oakham
7) All Saints, Brixworth
8) St Edmund's, Warkton
9) St Andrew's, Cotterstock
10) St Peter's, Raunds
11) St Mary and All Saints, Nassington
12) St Andrew's, Barnwell
13) St Peter's, Lowick
14) St Matthew's, Langford
15) St Mary's, Swinbrook
16) St Barnabas, Oxford
17) St Mary's, Bampton
18) St Philip and St James, Oxford
19) All Saints, Nuneham Courtenay

EAST ANGLIA

East of the Roman Ermine Street is this land of fen, flint and chalk, of estuaries and the long sea-fishing coast. It is a flat land with tall limestone and worn sandstone churches and circular towers always in sight, an undramatic land where the sky is the landscape and where monks have settled on little low islands. Sequestered villages cluster round wide greens, red-brick outhouses, weather-boarded cottages reed-thatched and colour-washed; it is a country where one is charmed to be lost. Edward VII led holiday-makers to the sandy coast and Arthur Ransome lured them to the Broads. Yet it still remains isolated today.

1) St Botolph's, Boston
2) St Wendreda's, March
3) St Mary's, West Walton
4) Walpole St Peter's
5) Pembroke College Chapel, Cambridge
6) Ely Cathedral
7) St Nicholas's, King's Lynn
8) St Faith's, Little Witchingham
9) Binham Priory
10) St Margaret's, Cley-next-the-Sea
11) St Andrew's, Gunton
12) St Michael and All Angels, Booton
13) Norwich Cathedral
14) The Old Meeting House, Norwich
15) The Octagon, Norwich
16) St Andrew's, North Lopham
17) Holy Trinity, Long Melford
18) Walpole Old Chapel, Ipswich
19) St John's, Thaxted
20) St John's, Finchingfield
21) St Mary's, Great Warley
22) St Laurence's, Blackmore

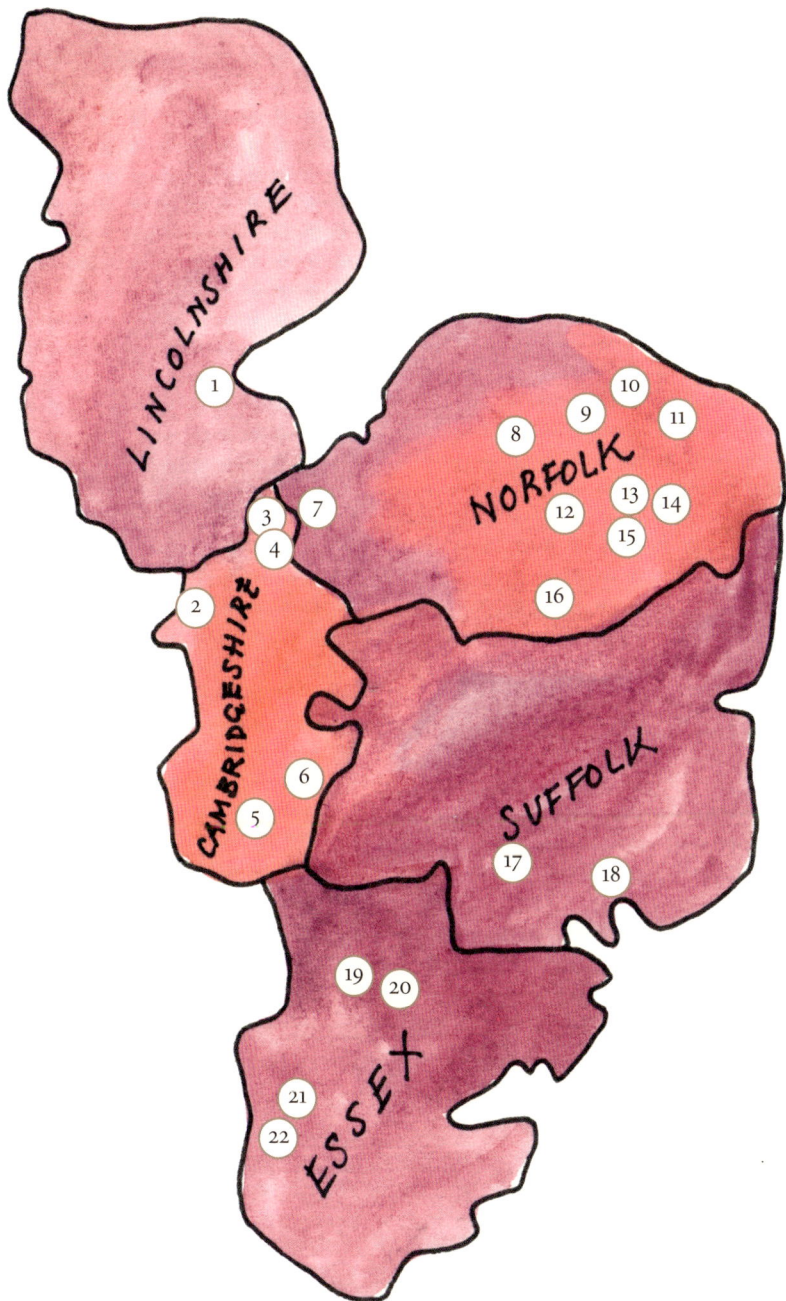

The SOUTH

The White Cliffs are an invading mariner's ever-fixed mark, and that chalk ridge leads through the Garden of England to the heart of the Home Counties. Along the coast is the charmingly desolate Romney Marsh, home to half a dozen lovely silent churches; to the north, the dry sandy pines fringe the south edges of expanded London. Pilgrims to St Swithun and St Thomas encounter every style of English architecture profusely represented and of the highest quality. The green and pleasant land supports villages and churches where the stone ranges through all the colours of the rainbow to brown and grey, reflecting the varied geology.

1) Holy Trinity, Theale
2) St Mary's, Langley Marish
3) St Lawrence's, Alton
4) St Mary's, Hartley Wespall
5) St Mary's, West Cowes, Isle of Wight
6) St Bartholomew's, Fingest
7) Friends Meeting House, Jordans
8) St Andrew by the Wardrobe, City
9) St Paul's, Covent Garden
10) St George's, Bloomsbury
11) Westminster Cathedral
12) United Reformed Church, Clapton Park
13) St John's, Hackney
14) Christ Church, Spitalfields
15) St Peter's, Chiswick
16) St Lawrence Jewry, City
17) St Mary Woolnoth, City
18) St Hubert's, Idsworth
19) St Paul's, Stansted Chapel
20) All Saints, Woodchurch
21) St Nicholas's, New Romney

BERKSH

H

BUCKINGHAMSHIRE

BEDS

HERTS

10 11
9   14
8   13 17
12 16
15

6   7

2

LONDON

KENT

20

21

4

SURREY

SUSSEX

18

19

THE WEST

From Stonehenge westwards through chalk and clay to the granite and slate on the coast, this land is heathery hills and prehistoric earthworks. The people worked in slate-grey fishing ports, tin mines, water-powered mills and lush valleys where wool meant huge resources for church building. Along lanes of hydrangea and fuchsia lie cob-walled, thickly thatched bartons and magnificent church towers with their wide chancel screens and their six bells ringing out over modest houses of Ham and Beer stone with stone-tiled roofs. There are 250 miles of coastal path circling a landscape where artists and craftsmen have revelled and still come for inspiration.

1) St Protus and St Hyacinth, Blisland
2) St Swithin's, Launcells
3) St Mary's, Molland
4) St Andrew's, Cullompton
5) St John's, Ashton
6) St Andrew's, Ipplepen
7) St Winifred's, Branscombe
8) St Mary's, Isle Abbotts
9) St John's, Yeovil
10) St Mary Redcliffe, Bristol

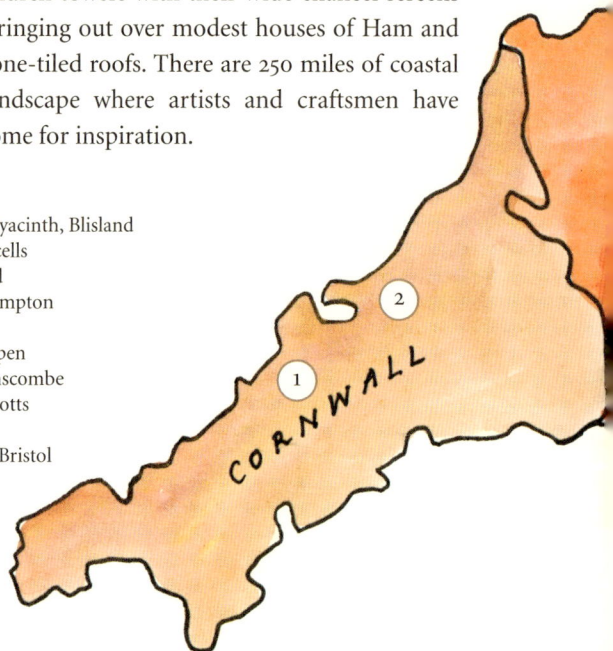

CORNWALL

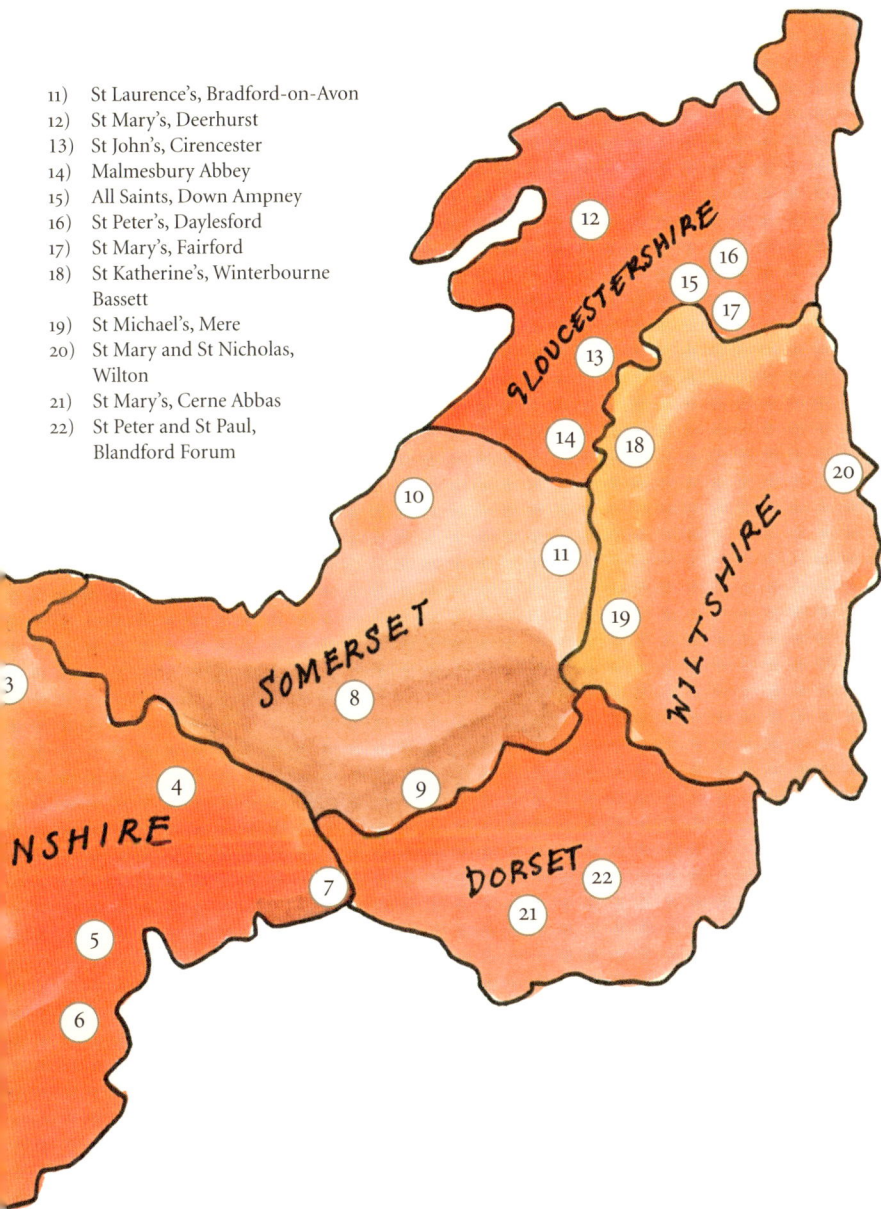

GLOUCESTERSHIRE

SOMERSET

WILTSHIRE

DORSET

...NSHIRE

MONUMENTS

A monument is a reminder, commemorating the dead. Most commonly found in churches today are tablets, attached to the wall or to pillars, with facts of identity: dates of birth and death, place of residence, and perhaps some praise, maybe even something of the tragic nature of death. Effigies, which are often of more interest to those of us who come after, have always been more costly.

A chapel full of monuments leaps the fetters of period and style. There might be pious memorials linking neighbours or members of the same family to each other, even if they died centuries apart. Thus in terms of church-as-a-record-of-social-history, it is often its monuments that are the most telling element of the whole building.

Monuments display the best-quality workmanship of their time, as well as bolder experimentation than in the church proper. This idea that the church monument is a miniaturised grand architectural project is borne out all over the country; on the crocketted confection of Edward II's tomb in Gloucester Cathedral, the Decorated-style nodding ogees and pinnacles are stacked in a way that could not be realised elsewhere in the church, not least because of cost. It is possible to build a tomb to a far higher specification than its background simply because it is smaller.

Because the monument can function as a CRUCIBLE OF NEW IDEAS (Death where is thy sting...?), it is unsurprising that the first evidence of our adoption of the European Renaissance is to be seen in the canopies and temple fronts of sixteenth-century funerary compositions. There are the Classical orders and, with them, the volutes and acanthus scrolls, the dentils and the egg and dart, the Vitruvian scroll, and the reeded and fluted columns that went on to become the *lingua franca* of European architecture for three hundred years. They were used for the first time in Britain on tombs. Those polychrome monuments with obedient black-coated children and ruffled and martingaled wives shout 'You saw it first HERE!'

Medieval tombs are, in some ways, simpler than later ones. Few effigies show emotion, and they are more like death masks than portraits – perhaps, indeed, the effigy was never intended to be a likeness, but rather a symbol. Costume and, frequently, armour seem important, an indicator of status.

Brass plaques, known as 'brasses', appear from the thirteenth century; the oldest one extant is of Sir John D'Abernon (1277) in St Mary's Church at Stoke D'Abernon, Surrey. Brasses often celebrate a military knight who, like the stone knight (1280) of Dorchester Abbey, Oxfordshire, is dramatically tense and ready to spring up and defend himself and his Church, his sword held ready in his hand. Poverty, dishonesty and OPPORTUNISM have led to many brasses being stolen, leaving only a ghost-brass impression in a slab: a figure, a shield or two and a swag where the name was once engraved.

Monuments are housed on the wall or are free-standing, and they are everywhere. The early Church discouraged burial within the church building, but abbots and bishops, then knights and temporal lords, soon colonised the naves, chapels and cloisters. Initially, they lay exposed on a stone slab, shield or coffin with minimal decoration, but, by the late thirteenth century, grandees frequently lay beneath a vaulted canopy. The Talbot tomb in Bampton Church, Oxfordshire (c.1350) is a good example of this in Decorated style. A straight-sided pointed arch springs from two beautifully carved, crowned head-stops with sharply delineated hair and beard (the latter is on the male head only).

The Talbot tomb lies decently in the north transept, whereas the Fettiplace tombs in St Mary's Church of Swinbrook, Oxfordshire, line the whole chancel, making it their own with an admirably full-blooded possessiveness. The tombs begin with Elizabethan experimental Renaissance Classicism (1613) then pass through a rumbustious form of seventeenth-century Baroque (1686), before arriving with imperial Roman confidence in the mid-eighteenth century (1743). It is a PROPRIETORIAL LAND GRAB by the dead that underpins their descendants' status down the generations.

It is more usual to find a family grouping in a chantry chapel. This would often be a later addition to the church building, the gift of a prelate or lord whose bequest not only funded the extension's construction, but endowed a foundation that would ensure the saying of masses perpetual to the memory of the deceased. These arrangements were brought to an unceremonious halt during the Reformation: they smacked of murky religious superstition and they immobilised sizeable sums of capital. Some of the most finely wrought late-Gothic workmanship can be found in these buildings, and perhaps grandest of all is the Beauchamp Chapel at St Mary's Warwick (1443–64). Here, power of national significance is robed in appropriately regal togs; fan vaults and panelling are mere backgrounds for the stupendous tombs of the Beauchamps, Dudleys and Fulkes.

In some places, the dead seem likely to outnumber the congregation. St Mary's Church at Harefield, Middlesex, is crowded with monuments. It is more like the Soane Museum, that most idiosyncratic ACCUMULATION OF ANTIQUARIAN REMAINS, sarcophagi and paintings in Lincoln's Inn Fields, London, than a parish church. The Countess of Derby (1637) lies by a four-poster bed, near where the master carver Grinling Gibbons has given us another, more comfortable-looking lady in a loose Roman robe (1692). Also joggling each other are tombs by John Michael Rysbrack (1727) and John Bacon (1800), plus Jacobean monuments in glorious polychrome. To worship here is to be in the company of a cloud of witnesses from across seven centuries.

The Georgians often dressed their figures in contemporary clothing or draped them in Classical dress – a toga or the armour of the legions. Roman and Greek costume needled its way into contemporary dress in the early nineteenth century, when breast-grazing muslins drove Regency bucks to distraction, so it is no surprise to see it clothing the idealised dead. In the skilful hand of John Flaxman and his school of late-eighteenth-century sculpture, the deceased are draped in exceptionally lifelike marble folds.

Sentiment, so much set aside before, creeps in charmingly to Penelope Boothby's memorial in Ashbourne (1793). The inscription BREAKS THE HEART: 'She was in form and intellect most exquisite. The unfortunate parents ventured their all on this frail bark. And the wreck was total.' And contrasting with the staidness of most tombs is that of Lady Elizabeth Nightingale (died 1731) in Westminster Abbey. She was out walking when a flash of lightning so shocked her that she miscarried and died. Death, standing by us, has come from the opened vault to claim her, while her husband tries vainly to WARD OFF DEATH'S SPEAR.

The late seventeenth and early eighteenth centuries were the age of lettering. Obfuscatory archaic script was eclipsed by bold Roman lettering, copied from Trajan's Column of ancient Rome. The austere letter forms are wrought by the local mason's chisel into idiosyncrasies. Letters drop from upper case to lower; an 'e' will shelter beneath a capital T's bar in a space-saving economy that became characteristic of the period. The rule is often still visible, scratched into slate or marble; there is a done-yesterday immediacy about these inscriptions that gives emotional weight to the content. In the second half of the eighteenth century this wide-eyed unselfconsciousness was lost: only curlicues and swaggings, or carefully carved death's heads, save these inscriptions from dreary conformity.

Although they were less elaborate, being monuments to lesser men, eighteenth- and nineteenth-century graves outside the church chased the same stylistic hares as inside: Classical ornament and varying scripts. Among the graves of the Ebenezers, Abners and Ezekiels (the Old Testament obviously held great sway among the child-bearing plough-folk of that era) are the poignant, tiny, children's graves, as significant an outlay for their grieving parents as any iron-fenced mausoleum inside the church. But, with few exceptions, churchyard monuments are the lesser form.

Within the church, a particular mason might devote himself to a church and his preferences, perhaps *putti* (were they his own children, who had no memorial?), or fronds of palm and festoons, would come to dominate the place. Over time, tablets in marble or finest limestone gained and lost pediments and architraves as fashion moved on. LUSTY, SAUSAGE-THICK swirls and baroqueries were refined to Palladian order and restraint, became frivolous again, then slumped into the grim-faced Gothic style of the nineteenth century. These later monuments reflect the increasing impact of Empire and the outward-facing nature of every parish in Britain. Deaths violent or pathetic in palm-strewn strands or humid jungle were marked with matter-of-fact wording, as were the casualties of wars on the North-West Frontier (might sound familiar) and in Africa.

But it was the Boer War in 1899–1902 and, hot on its heels, the mass slaughter of the First World War in 1914–18 that introduced the war memorial to the church. War memorials come in many forms, from white marble rectangles, perhaps watched over by an angel, to banner-racked chapels recording the deaths of entire regiments. A generation of men – from the sons of the big house or rectory to the children of the gardener, herdsman or miner – flooded the community of souls commemorated. The lists of the Fallen, read out each year on Remembrance Sunday, unbalanced the roll-call of centuries.

TOMB OF Sir JOHN GERMAN
ST PETER'S · LOWICK
NORTHAMPTONSHIRE

BALUSTER

BRASSES

brass of jolly good fellow who died about 1400. check tonsure

GREEN TOMB · ST PETER'S
LOWICK · NORTHAMPTONSHIRE

POLYCHROME
REPRESENTATIONS
of FAMILY

STRAPWORK
DECORATION

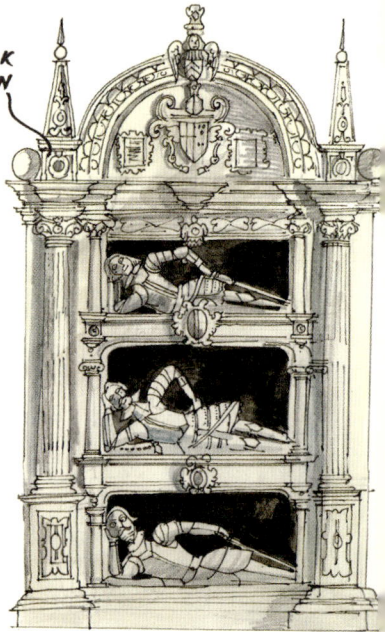

ST MARY'S
LANGLEY MARISH
BERKSHIRE

ST MARY'S
SWINBROOK
OXFORDSHIRE

FETCHING RUFFS

Parnel   Malin   Ioane   Anne   Oliph   Rob
                            Eliz

PULVINATED FRIEZE

PEDIMENT

FRIEZE

CONSOLE

VOLUTE

SHIELDS

NICHE

GLASS

The history of stained glass relies upon the history of windows. Saxon windows were hardly wider than arrow slits and often not glazed. Greater piercing into walls allowed taller, wider lancet windows in Early English churches. Two lancets side by side under a common arch might have a roundel, like fretwork, between and above them. If the roundel was reinforced with four cusps, the resulting shape was a 'quatrefoil'. A single, wide lancet might include simple Y-tracery, which later led to the more refined bar tracery.

A further, logical development in Gothic design was the introduction of RETICULATED TRACERY. (Reticulated means 'resembling a net'. This unusual adjective comes up again in the 'reticulated giraffe', whose skin is decorated in a net-pattern, cream on chestnut; also, a reticule is a net bag. Now you will never forget.) This flowing tracery produced new shapes and, thus, new architectural terms: mouchettes, daggers, tears and flame-like forms.

The method of filling windows with pieces of coloured glass came to England via France before the Conquest of 1066. It was as dramatic a leap forward as the change from printed photograph to iPad has been today, making images of illuminated-manuscript quality available to every churchgoer for the first time. As the Norman style moved into Gothic, church walls, often brightly painted, became animated by glass visions and Biblical scenes.

Production techniques hardly changed over the next four hundred years, except for the subtle variation of new colours. Colour, introduced using metallic oxides, was generally fired into the glass itself: copper and iron for red, cobalt for blue, manganese for purple and copper for green. The master glazier would make a full-sized drawing of the subject, then lay the coloured pieces over this 'cartoon', before joining them with strips of lead, called 'calmes'. These became as visually dominant as the glass.

The growing desire to bring in more light led to the introduction of unstained areas of 'white' glass. However, what was intended to be white glass was often light grey, giving rise to the monochromatic 'grisailles' at Salisbury Cathedral (c.1225) and at the Chapter House in York (from 1270). Early in the fourteenth century, glaziers discovered that treating white glass with silver sulphide could produce a yellow or deep orange tint, giving saints their halos and kings their crowns. White glass could be painted, as are the landscapes and architecture on windows at King's College Chapel, Cambridge (1515–31).

The windows at Fairford in Gloucestershire (1500–17) are the star and climax of all parish church stained glass. Within a framework of large Perpendicular windows, this glass depicts the ENTIRE CATHOLIC FAITH on a series of bright and broad glass canvases.

There was little new glass made in the seventeenth and eighteenth centuries, when Classicism and plain glass reigned supreme, although roundels from Holland were sometimes set into plain windows and, in 1785, a Nativity in the chapel of New College, Oxford was painted from a design by Joshua Reynolds. By the nineteenth century, there was a renewed enthusiasm for medieval glazing, and Gothic Revival churches were once again aflame with colour blazing through the new windows.

S·CATHERINE

ST MARY'S · FAIRFORD
GLOUCESTERSHIRE

fairly full-on Oxford Movement
imagery

AUMBRY

PULPIT
ST BARNABAS'S
OXFORD

EARLY ORGAN c.1450

PEW ENDS-
POPPY-HEAD

INTERIOR FITTINGS

The furnishings of a church are as much a focus for craftsmanship and creativity as the building itself. Some, such as fonts, are common to all churches, but others are date-specific (lecterns appeared only in the fifteenth century). These items are all of liturgical use and to fully comprehend a church it is important to know about them.

At the entrance to a church, there might be a HOLY WATER STOUP filled with consecrated water. Parishioners dip their fingers in the water on entering the church and sign themselves with the cross as a reminder of their BAPTISM in the FONT. Significantly, this is also near the entrance, because baptism is the welcoming into the church. In the past, covers would have kept the water clean and prevented it from being stolen for irreligious purposes. There are

still some wonderful FONT CANOPIES, carpentry masterworks that reach high to the roof and are lifted up by means of a pulley.

PEWS were a comparatively late introduction. Originally, seating was, at best, an unobtrusive stone bench where the weakest would go to rest. In the Middle Ages there were wooden benches; the BENCH ENDS were sometimes decorated with figures, window-style tracery or coats of arms, but more common were the POPPY-HEAD carvings (from French *poupée*, doll) in the form of a fleur-de-lys. BOX PEWS were brought in during the seventeenth century, with doors to protect against draughts. More usual now are Victorian pine pews with a ledge for kneeling; Victorians would have drawn a comfortable warmth from enormous tortoise stoves in the church. In a church chancel, there may be STALLS facing each other, as in a college or monastery, perhaps sporting MISERICORDS for monks to lean upon when standing during long services. These can be carved with scenery, people, creatures or caricatures, usually invisible unless the misericords are turned up for use.

PULPIT refers to the place in a parish church from where the sermon is delivered. There are some medieval pulpits, but James I's canon that the Bible should be read in every church instigated a frantic building of new ones. Many we see today date from the seventeenth century. A two-decker pulpit allowed the parson to read from the lower desk and ascend to preach. It sometimes had an hour-glass within, which did not necessarily denote long sermons; the 1867 glass in the Chapel Royal of the Savoy ran for only eighteen minutes. The familiar desk-top or book-rest LECTERNS in the form of an eagle made of wood or brass usually date from 1400.

Frequently the victim of Reformation ICONOCLASM (smashing for reasons of dogma), WALL-PAINTINGS are often more restored than original. Square or lozenge-shaped HATCHMENTS are painted armorial bearings of deceased parishioners or Royal coats of arms. Over the chancel arch, there are occasionally the remains of a fine DOOM, representing the Last Judgment with the splendidly miserable Wicked being pulled down to Hell's teeth by fierce devils.

The bread, wine and water for a Communion service are kept on a CREDENCE TABLE. The valuable Communion vessels may be kept in a cabinet called an AUMBRY. Facing this, usually on the south wall, the priest will have a basin known as a PISCINA to wash his hands and to clean the vessels. The piscina is often built into the SEDILIA, the seats for the celebrant and presiding priests. A REREDOS is a wallpiece behind the ALTAR, originally made of painted stone. A SQUINT or hagioscope is a small opening cut through the chancel arch or wall to enable worshippers to see the Elevation of the Host from outside or from the aisle.

A medieval SCREEN once separated the chancel from the rest of the building. Most screens that you will find now date from the fifteenth and early sixteenth centuries. They were often sturdy enough to carry a LOFT for a choir or organ, and they could provide access to the ROOD. This rood was a crucifix flanked by the Virgin Mary and St John, and it stood high and commanding, which rendered it vulnerable to the destructive reformers of the 1500s.

REIGNS OF KINGS & QUEENS

PERPENDICULAR

Edward III (1327–1377)
Richard II (1377–1399)
Henry IV (1399–1413)
Henry V (1413–1422)
Henry VI (1422–1461)
Edward IV (1461–1483)
Richard III (1483–1485)
Henry VII (1485–1509)

SAXON & NORMAN

Alfred (871–899)
Edward the Elder (899–924)
Athelstan (924–939)
Edmund (939–946)
Eadred (946–955)
Eadwig (955–959)
Edgar (959–975)
Edward the Martyr (975–979)
Aethelred II (979–1016)
Canute (1016–1035)
Harold (1035–1040)
Harthcanute (1040–1042)
Edward the Confessor (1042–1066)
William I (1066–1087)
William II (1087–1100)
Henry I (1100–1135)
Stephen (1135–1154)
Henry II (1154–1189)
Richard I (1189–1199)

EARLY ENGLISH

John (1199–1216)

DECORATED

Henry III (1216–1272)
Edward I (1272–1307)
Edward II (1307–1327)

BAROQUE & GOTHIC SURVIVAL

Henry VIII (1509–1547)
Edward VI (1547–1553)
Mary I (1553–1558)
Elizabeth I (1558–1603)
James I (1603–1625)
Charles I (1625–1649)
Commonwealth (1649–1660)
Charles II (1660–1685)
James II (1685–1688)
William and Mary (1689– 1702)
Anne (1702–1714)

GEORGIAN

George I (1714–1727)
George II (1727–1760)
George III (1760–1820)

REGENCY & VICTORIAN

George IV (1820–1830)
William IV (1830–1837)
Victoria (1837–1901)

MODERN

Edward VII (1901–1910)
George V (1910–1936)
Edward VIII (1936–1936)
George VI (1936–1952)
Elizabeth II (1952–present)

INDEX OF PEOPLE

Page numbers in *italic* refer
to illustrations

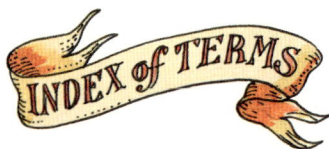

INDEX of TERMS

sanctuary *20*, 156, 157
Saxons *19*, 31–4, 207
sconces 118
scotia fillet *26*
screens 215
  Baroque *104–5*
  chancel 117
  exterior 48–9
  Gothic Revival 133
  low *21*
  Modern 157
  parclose 99
  rood *21*, 64–5, *89*, 98, 117,
    133
scrolls *107*, *109*, 198
sedilia 64, *71*, 133, 215
Serlian windows *124*
sermons 214
set-offs *19*
shafts *26*
  clustered 49, *52*, *57*
  Norman 35
  Perpendicular 84
  vault *22*
  Victorian *153*
shelters *126*
shields 205
sills *106*
Society for the Protection of
  Ancient Buildings 145
spandrels *19*, 82, *91*
spirelets 64
spires: broached *135*, *136*, 142
  crocketted *19*, *86*
  Modern 155
  Victorian *135*, *136*, 143, *151*,
    155
  see also steeples
springing: arches *72*
  vaulting *22*, *23*, 35, 84
squint 215
stained glass 49, 133, 143, 157,
  207–8, *209–11*
staircases 132
stalls 214
stations of the Cross *139*
statuary 64, *138*, 141, 200
steel 156, 157
steeples 133, 142, 155
  see also spires
stilted arches *17*, *149*
stole 144
storeys 14
stoups, holy water 213
stoves 214
strapwork *204*
string course 36, *55*, 68, *134*
struts *16*
stylobate *137*

tablets 197, 201
tears 207
testers *21*, 99
thurifer 132
tie beams *16*
tiercerons *23*, *94*
tiles 142
tombs 10–11, 83, 198–201, *202–5*
torus *26*
Tournai marble 35, *38*
towers 14, *19*, *20*
  bell *158*
  Commissioners' churches
    130
  crossing 35, 50
  Early English *61*
  Perpendicular 85
  Victorian *135*, 143, *147*, 155
tracery 14, *18*, 207
  Decorated 67, *72–3*
  Early English *56–7*, 66–7
  Perpendicular 82, 84, *90*
  Victorian *135*, *136*, *150*, *153*
Tractarianism 143
transepts 117
transoms *18*, 82, 84
transverse ribs *23*, 51
trefoils 14, *18*, *56*, *70*, *91*, *92*
triforium 50, 83
triglyphs *137*
trumpet moulding *59*
trusses *16*, 156
turrets 84
Tuscan order *27*
tympanum *40*, *108*, *137*

Unitarians 119, 143–4

vanes *19*, *86*, *135*, *136*, *151*
vaulting 14, *22–3*
  barrel *22*, 35, 50, 51
  Decorated 65, 66
  Early English 50–1
  fan 84, *94*, 199
  groin *22*, 35, 50, 51
  liernes *23*, 65, 66, *94*
  Norman 50
  Perpendicular 84, *94*
Venetian windows *124*
vermiculation 15
vesica windows *52*
vestments 133, 144
vicars 119
Victorian architecture 129–33,
  134–9, 141–5, *146–53*
Vikings 33–4, 35
Vitruvian scrolls 198
volutes *25*, *27*, 198, *205*
voussoirs *42*, *106*, 142

walls: Georgian 117
  Gothic 47–8, 51
  Modern 155
  Norman 34–5, 47, 50
war memorials 201
weather table *19*
weather vanes *19*, *135*, *136*
web, vaulting 51
Wesleyanism 119
westworks 35
windows 14, *18–19*
  blind *52*
  Classical *106–7*
  clerestory *21*, *23*, 51, 84, *146*
  Decorated 67, *72–3*, 82
  Diocletian *121*
  dormer *148*
  Early English 51, *56–7*, 66–7, 207
  Georgian *124*
  grisailles 208
  lancets *17*, *18*, 49, *60*, 207
  lanterns 65, 69, *86*, 100
  Perpendicular *18*, 82, 84, *87*, *92–3*
  plate glass 157
  rose 133
  round-topped *43*
  Saxon *19*, 207
  Venetian *124*
  Victorian *135*, *136*
  see also stained glass; tracery
wine-glass pulpits 95

Y-tracery *18*, *57*, 207
Young England 131

THANKS

I have worked with Alastair Langlands on four books but none has relied on him as much as this one. He has driven the car as we visited churches round the country, and has recorded, edited and contributed at every level. So my gratitude to him is total. Barely a church visited failed to elicit a 'been here before in ... 1965/1995/2005' response, and his prodigious memory has been vital.

This and its predecessor, *Rice's Architectural Primer*, are the unruly children of an idea of Jeremy Musson, then architectural editor of *Country Life* magazine. Its editor, Mark Hedges, and current Architectural Editor, John Goodall, have kindly allowed me to use some illustrations originally published by them here.

Richard Atkinson at Bloomsbury and Caroline Dawnay at United Agents both shaped the book and then made sure that I stuck to the plot, if not the schedule. Xa Shaw Stewart has edited in a way probably more structural than any editor would choose; and Octavia Pollock has then ploughed through the legions of inaccuracies and omissions kindly and cleverly. Peter Dawson at Grade has designed this book as beautifully as the last. That then is the team required by an author whose other working life has been rather fractured by writing another book. So endless gratitude is owed to – and forbearance received from – Matthew, Julia, Caryl and Leigh at Emma Bridgewater. Thank you.

And my inadequate thanks and love go to Will Whittaker and Lucy Catling. Will has ordered, transformed and corralled my illustrations into this book. His wizardry, total good humour and grace are beyond any expectations. Lucy has looked after me, and the sometimes baffling text, throughout the last year, and knows more about crocketted pinnacles than she ever expected she would need to.

Lastly Emma, who has visited yet more churches, gone to bed to the sound of the Archers omnibus on Radio 4's 'Listen Again' at a time it was never intended to be listened to, and accepted the disruption that another book causes. Thank you most of all.